# TAKE LIFE BY THE HELM!

## Proven Strategies For Gaining Control

*How To Live A Courageous,*
*Adventurous And Deliberate Life*

## Doug Nielsen
*The Take Ownership Specialist*

Dedicated To

*God and my four beautiful children.*

# TAKE LIFE BY THE HELM

Take Life By The Helm: *Proven Strategies for Gaining Control*
Copyright ©2014 by Doug Nielsen
Fourth Edition

ISBN: 978-0-615-29332-5
$15.00

Published by:
DNC Publishing
P.O. Box 150526, Ogden, UT 84415

Printed and bound in the United States of America.

**Credits**
Cover Design: Peter Giordano
Text Design: Eric Barkle
Edited by: Peter Giordano

Doug Nielsen
P.O. Box 150042, Ogden, UT 84415
www.DougSpeaks.com
Doug@DougSpeaks.com

# CONTENTS

# ACKNOWLEDGEMENTS:

I thank God for the wonderful opportunity He's afforded me to live, love and learn. I thank my wife for unending support and her listening to all my harebrained ideas all these years. I love you. I thank my kids who still acknowledge me as their father...*even in public.* I love you and couldn't be more proud of each of you. I want to thank my mom for the amazing example she set for me.

A big thanks goes to Melanie who, without her encouragement, support and advice, this book would have never been printed. Thank you! I thank Peter Giordano for his brilliance in making this come to life and Ralph Johnson for his insightful input. I express my deepest gratitude for the impact that Viktor Frankl had on my life and for his willingness to love, inspire and uplift! I express my love and gratitude for Tim Border—thanks for believing in me and lifting me to where I would have never gotten without you. I give praise to Craig Berthold, for without your insight and profound influence I would have never pursued my dreams.

Lastly, I thank you for reading this book to help better yourself, your family and our world! May God Bless You in the pursuit of your purpose and dreams.

# INTRODUCTION:

Along the lines of what Helen Keller said, the most daring adventure of all is saying "yes" to *your* life.

I've yet to meet a person who just wanted to live a mediocre life and then die. Yet somehow, in some way, we can all be lulled into an almost catatonic state of exhaustion, boredom, numbness, apathy, stress, anger, jealousy, resentment and despair. And, by letting this happen, we say "no" to our lives.

A lot of us do, in fact. A *www.monster.com* survey showed that a stunning 81% of respondents felt that their lives were way out of balance.

It can be so easy to lose your heart and courage and let your passions wither away. And when that happens, many of us desperately attempt to fill the accompanying void with distractions like "electronic heroin" (TV, Internet, games), work, shopping, and various other addictions. With our passions gone, we try to numb ourselves to cope with what's left in our lives.

It can become a vicious cycle.

But...*is this why you're alive?*

Are you living the life you know your Creator intended for you? Is your purpose yet to be fulfilled? Is your existence a compelling adventure that enlists your courage, creativity and strength for a cause outside yourself? Or are you just living paycheck to paycheck, not just financially, but mentally, physically and spiritually, too?

Fortunately, there is good news: Life still holds great promise for you...*but you have to first realize that you already have what you need to succeed!*

You are enough, *as is*, yet you can always learn, grow and improve. Dormant inside you is a power beyond belief. Beyond description. My goal is to help you awaken this tremendous force.

You're not on this earth to cower and play it small. You're here to enrich the world with your talents and skills. It's my hope, as you read this book and share it with others, that you'll stir the "remembrance" of your own greatness and power. And that you'll start questioning yourself.

For example, why are you working where you are? For just a paycheck? Or because you love it? Or...is it just a stepping stone to something far greater? Can you see the bigger picture of your life? Is it a life of significance where you're growing and contributing despite the massive storms you face?

*Are you a deliberate force for good?*

I want you to wake up and give a wholehearted "YES" to your life...and that's exactly what this book is designed to help you do.

*This is your time and your place to launch a glorious new start!* You can begin today to shed yourself of blame, of victim mentality, excuses, rationalizations and start rising to a greatness your Creator always intended for you. This book will teach you how to finally *Take Life by the Helm,* how to let your *North Star* give you the daily inspiration you need, and how to be guided, in detail, to your own version of success by your *Lighthouse.*

**Think of this as the owner's manual for your life…the one nobody ever gave you before.**

While you're on this personal journey of yours, feel free to e-mail me at *doug@dougspeaks.com.* And visit *www. dougspeaks.com* where you can sign up for *Doug's Daily Dose of Power* and my monthly newsletter *Take Life by the Helm in 59 Seconds or Less.*

Remember…*a ship is safe in the harbor, but that's not what ships were meant to be.*

So let's set sail for your TRUE life and the amazing journey of discovery and adventure ahead of you.

Doug

*"The greatest day of your life is the day that you decide that your life is your own, that ultimately you are at The Helm. This awesome journey called life is yours, and you are responsible for the quality of it. Saying 'yes' to this Provident journey is the most important 'yes' you can give. Rising above and being worthy of your challenges is the greatest honor that can be bestowed. This is life. Live each moment with dignity here and now!"*

—Doug Nielsen—

# Chapter 1

# WAKE UP
# AND SET SAIL

You can sometimes see it in the eyes of those around you: That vacant, distant, somewhat bombed-out stare.

And you can sometimes hear it in their words. They avoid absolutes when talking about their plans, their dreams, what they'd like to do. There are too many "ifs." Too many "maybes." Too many "some days."

Way too many "I don't knows."

What's going on here? A contagious disease? Some mysterious epidemic that's gone unreported in the media?

## Their Eyes Tell The Story

No. The sad truth is your loved ones and co-workers— most of the people you come in contact with, in fact— *have simply lost control.*

They've lost control of their lives. *Poof!* If they ever really had it in the first place.

And the grim reality is, *they know all about it.*

These are people who aren't where they thought they'd be by now. Or achieved anywhere near what they hoped they'd achieve. Few conquests animate their faces during the day. Their lives simply don't mesh with the spectacular dreams of their youth.

And they have no idea what to do about it. That's the thing. Time is passing them by, and they can't figure out how to right the ship.

That's what you're seeing in their eyes.

Having said that...

## What Do People See When They Look In *Your* Eyes?

That's really the question, isn't it?

Does confidence come beaming out of your baby blues?

Do people see ironclad purpose in there?

Determination and courage? Passion and compassion?

Does excitement and humor dance in your pupils?

Or...are your eyes...*just like everyone else's?*

Are you seen as just another person living a life of, as Thoreau so eloquently put it, "quiet desperation"?

## The Real You Is Waiting Deep Down Inside

It's not your fault, you know. Not really. At least, it hasn't been, up to this page anyway.

Down deep inside, you've probably realized that there's a whole lot more to your life. **But no one's ever shown you how to access it. No one's ever taught you how to bring it to the surface.**

*No one's ever handed you an instruction manual, in other words.*

So there, inside, the real you sits...waiting patiently... ready for a day that may never, ever come.

There are times when you may even catch a glimpse of your real self. There's that longing to be the person you always intended to be...those wonderful gifts and talents you see quietly rusting inside...the courage you need to live a magnificent life...the eagerness to achieve the success of a lifetime.

But then, by stark contrast, there's your present-day reality. The job you couldn't care less about...the dull monotony of your everyday routine...your safety and complete lack of risk-taking...the way you blame and criticize others without giving it a second thought.

**It's a life the *real you* pretty much despises.**

Another life is waiting.

It's a life of excitement...of victories and defeats...of the same kind of exhilaration you'd feel if you were up there in the crow's nest of an ancient tall ship, surveying the spectacular sea, feeling the delightful sting of ocean wind in your grinning face.

Speaking of the sea, maybe you've heard that a ship is safest in the harbor...but that's not where a ship is meant to be.

A ship is meant to be out there on the ocean, propelled by the wind, slicing through the waves, braving the storms, crossing the sea en route to exciting ports.

Okay...but...aren't there risks out there on the ocean? *Sure.* Couldn't something go wrong on the high seas? *Of course.* Isn't it possible that you could even, worst-case scenario, *sink?*

*Yes, sinking in the middle of the ocean is a distinct possibility.*

*"I've continued to recognize the power individuals have to change virtually anything and everything in their lives in an instant. I've learned that the resources we need to turn our dreams into reality are within us, merely waiting for the day when we decide to wake up and claim our birthright."*

—Anthony Robbins—

But couldn't you also **face down all those threats and obstacles on the way to having the absolute adventure of a lifetime?**

*YES!!!*

Well, here's some breaking news: **The real you is just aching, screaming even, to have an adventure like that!**

Here's a story you need to hear, something that happened to me…

## Get Your Freak On

It was like a place you'd only see in the movies. The clear, turquoise water, gentle rush of the waves and warm sand between my toes left me feeling like I never wanted to leave.

As I walked along the beach, I stopped to look at a local vendor's wares.

This particular guy was barefoot and shirtless with long dreadlocks that looked like they hadn't been washed since the last episode of *Seinfeld.* He said "ya mon" after every sentence, and that was timed with a rhythmic nod of the head.

I told him I was looking for the right souvenir to remind me of my time in Belize.

He smiled and said, "My friend, your worries are over." For some reason, that didn't reassure me.

He came around the table and stood by me. "I have the perfect ting for ya, mon." He then picked up a Tiki mask, held it up to my face and in a soft yet intent voice said, "Look at dat, can you see it, mon? Can you hear whaditz saying to you?"

I started edging away, wondering what the guy was smoking. Or drinking. Or smoking *and* drinking. That was before things got...well...*really weird*.

He came so close to me I thought he was going to give me a kiss (and his breath was anything but minty fresh). He looked right into my eyes—right into my soul, seemingly—and, holding the mask up, asked if I could, "Hear it?"

"Hmmm. No. Can't say I hear anything at all."

Then he asked if the mask carving was asleep or awake.

"Well, if I had to guess, I'd say this pricy piece of carved wood looks asleep to me. But I don't..."

"Right, mon!"

He continued his disturbing gaze. Then: "This is the mask of the sleeping prince, and before he can become a king, he has to do what?"

Feeling all at once that this question had become significant, as if, in some fantastic, inexplicable way, my future hinged on me providing the right answer, I muttered...

"Wake up?"

"Yes, mon! Wake up! Like dis mask, you are a sleeping prince, and it is time for you to wake up. You must never forget dat you are one of God's beautiful creations. You are beautiful, mon! And you must now wake up to become the king you were born to be."

His words seemed to echo in my head long after he had finished speaking them. I felt frozen in place.

"You are here to do tings dat only you can do, mon!"

He then grabbed my hand, put it on my chest, and said, "You feel dat?"

I felt my heart. Yes, it was still beating.

"I do."

"Your heart beats today for a reason, and you must find out why. For it's dat 'why' dat will reveal your purpose. Your hell will be meeting, one day, the person you *could have been* and the contributions *you could have made.* **So wake up and become!**"

I was struggling to keep up.

He then asked in a suddenly accent-less, matter-of-fact way, "Now do you want the mask or not?"

I was momentarily speechless (which doesn't often happen to me). After fumbling for words, I managed, "Sure. I'll take it."

I had difficulty getting to sleep that night.

Lying there, I thought of the many people I'd known who had incredible gifts and potential, yet seemed forever mired in their lives.

They were my friend's sleeping princes.

And I couldn't help thinking of the people I'd known who we're doing wonderful things with their lives. These were the kings and queens he mentioned.

What I first deemed a "freaky situation" turned out to be one of the most powerful sermons I had ever heard.

*I was determined then and there, on that hotel bed in Belize, to finally wake up to my true self!*

## Three Metaphors To Help You Wake Up And Set Sail

Throughout the book, I'll be using three nautical concepts, three metaphors to help give you a clearer idea of how to gain control of your life and become your true self.

First is the concept of *The Helm*.

Second is the *North Star*.

Third is the *Lighthouse*.

Navigators of yesteryear, old captains at the helm, used the stars to chart their courses and make corrections along the way. Likewise, people who enjoy lives of greatness are not only at *The Helm* but, like those old-time mariners, have their own *North Star*, their own constant, to help get them where they're going, eventually being directed safely, and in detail, into the harbor by their *Lighthouse.*

Let's take a closer look at these concepts.

## First...*The Helm*...

So what exactly is *The Helm* in the context of this book?

*The Helm refers to you being in control.* It means using the power of your free will to deliberately choose your course no matter the circumstances. Being at *The Helm* means *you directing your thinking* to overcome the inevitable challenges that come your way.

Did you catch that? Directing your thinking? That means you actually being in charge of what goes through your mind.

What a concept. Your ultimate freedom depends on this. On grabbing *The Helm* and taking ownership and responsibility for your life without excuse, rationalization or blame.

This means living a life of honor grounded in truth and reality. *Reality?* That's the way things really are, not the fairy tale illusions we often construct.

While most everyone wants this—to be in control of their lives and live an honorable life—*few have any idea how to go about it.*

Fortunately, this book aims to teach you just that. Day by day. Year by year.

## Second...*Your North Star*...

The mariners did, of course, use stars to guide them toward their ports. You couldn't just pick up a GPS at your nearest RadioShack back then.

One star commonly used was the North Star. Why? Because it was and is a glorious *constant* in the sky. Mariners could count on it to direct them to where they wanted to go. But the use of this constant in their lives wasn't exactly a luxury.

It was, without any exaggeration, a matter of life or death.

Think about it. Old-time sailors were smack dab in the middle of the ocean, this endless watery expanse where nothing at all is stable, an environment that could change by the second. Yet, somehow, in some way, they learned to navigate this forlorn setting with precision.

All we can now say is, "Wow."

By connecting to the North Star they found a reliable, dependable way to get back to their lighthouses and ports, time after time.

So, okay, let's say you choose to take *The Helm* (assume ownership of your life while dispensing with the blame, the excuses and rationalizations), and you chart your course using the *North Star* (which means listening to your God, a higher power, your conscience, core values or your guiding principles).

In that case, so far so good.

The *North Star* is that loving voice inside you that's hopeful, reassuring, incredibly wise, astonishingly accurate—and, yes, sometimes really, really annoying—persistently nudging you towards doing those things you don't want to or don't know how to do.

The very same things that seem impossible, in other words.

Sadly, rather than take advantage of this wonderful asset, most of us spend our entire lives learning all the ways we can shut it up.

That ends here. On these pages, we'll help put you back in touch. You'll learn how to steer in the right direction for you, and you alone, using your own personal *North Star*.

Alright, next comes...

## Third...*Your Lighthouse*...

Once you start paying attention to it, your *North Star* will direct you right toward your own *Lighthouse*.

Your own "purposeful contribution," in other words.

Like a real-life lighthouse, your own *Lighthouse* will give you the *specific* direction, bearing and clarity you need to hone right in on your success.

In the same way a lighthouse shoots a powerful directional beam to mariners approaching the harbor, your *Lighthouse* will help spotlight your unique gifts, your greatest strengths (and weaknesses), and where you should go from here. And it will clearly separate the trivial and insignificant from your own personal brand of greatness...and shine light on the sacrifices it will take for you to achieve that greatness.

Combine all three metaphors—*The Helm*, your *North Star* and your *Lighthouse*—and you'll have a powerful formula for success, an unstoppable force for good.

That's what this book can give you.

## Caution: This Guide Book
## Is *Not* For Everyone

You probably should know that at the very start.

I didn't write this book to make you feel all warm and cozy.

Not that I'm trying to make this transformation particularly hard on you, understand. That's the last thing I want. It's just that sometimes, to get at the core truths of your life, you need to come face to face with realities that can be...well...*a bit disturbing*.

See, to accomplish great things, you need to get past your old, negative way of thinking. You've probably heard that saying, "if you always do what you've always done, you'll always get what you always got"?

That's why I'm challenging the way you do things. And think of things.

On the other hand, if you're just looking for a book that tells you I'm okay, you're okay, and everything in life is just peachy keen, here's my suggestion:

Close the book cover right now and place it in a spot where you won't likely come across it again for another year.

Maybe then you'll be better prepared to actually *own your own success*.

Seriously, and no offense at all intended, but you'll start moving ahead in your life only when you have the courage and commitment to take the next step. Maybe that sounds a bit trite and cliché.

It's true nonetheless.

*"It doesn't matter how long we may have been stuck in a sense of our limitations. If we go into a darkened room and turn on the light, it doesn't matter if the room has been dark for a day, a week, or ten thousand years—we turn on the light and it is illuminated. Once we control our capacity for love and happiness, the light has been turned on."*

—Sharon Salzberg—

There's the saying, "When student ready, teacher appear."

Hopefully, the book now in your hands is that teacher.

## My Promise To You

This book is dedicated *to helping you absolutely, positively seize control of your life for maybe the first time in your life.*

I promise to share all of my specific ideas, tips and techniques to help you seize life by *The Helm*. They've worked for literally thousands of people in the real world, as well as me.

You can also find a wealth of specific supportive material at *www.dougspeaks.com.*

Remember, I'm pulling for you here.

## From Your Darkest To Your Brightest Days

As a psychotherapist, executive coach, chief operating officer, husband, parent, son, karate guy, little league soccer coach, dog lover, fan of underdogs everywhere and, yes, taker-outer-of-the-trash, I've been on an adventure to learn how people from all walks of life find meaning and fulfillment under the most trying of circumstances.

I've worked with people in the darkest days of their lives where they could see no way out. There was the professional woman paralyzed by rage after the brutal rape and murder of her daughter...a dear friend who overcame a severe drug addiction that cost him his business and nearly his family...the parents gripped with despair because of the loss of their 21-year-old daughter due to medical negligence...the married couple so trapped by resentment and bitterness they couldn't even sit in the same room together…the overwhelming remorse a father had over the son who chose suicide… the woman who lost everything a mere 24 hours after her husband walked out on her.

Then there was the man with the million-dollar idea who would rather have his teeth yanked out by pliers, one at a time, and without anesthesia, than give a public presentation.

In each of these cases, my clients had reached a dead-end. They felt trapped and suffocated…yet somehow, against all odds, still managed to overcome their panic enough to prosper. They didn't just survive their challenges; they used their seemingly impossible circumstances to propel them to a greatness they could never, ever have imagined.

Now let's take a little voyage to Pirate Island and see what's going on there, okay?

---

*"Deep within man dwell those slumbering powers; powers that would astonish him, that he never dreamed of possessing, forces that would revolutionize his life if aroused and put into action."*

—Orison Swett Marden—

*"You are not here merely to make a living. You are here in order to enable the world to live more amply, with greater vision, with a finer spirit of hope and achievement. You are here to enrich the world and you impoverish yourself if you forget the errand."*

—Woodrow Wilson—

# Chapter 2

# ESCAPING ZOMBIES, SURVIVING MIND PIRATES

As mentioned in the last chapter, you can usually tell a lot about a person by the expression on his or her face.

Like it or not, our faces are usually windows to our souls, something that can be pretty hard to camouflage.

Try this experiment: Next time you're around lots of people, look at their faces (but, for safety's sake, please don't stare). What do their expressions and body language tell you?

What do their eyes say?

Can you see happiness? Sadness? Indifference?

*Or satisfaction, happiness and triumph?*

## Zombies Invade Cincinnati Airport!

While waiting in line to grab a sandwich at the Cincinnati airport, I had a conversation with a friendly airport worker.

In the course of our talk, he said, "Everyday I see zombies get off one plane and onto another. They all make zombie-like sounds and have the same lifeless expressions. I get a kick out of saying 'hi' just to see what they'll say back. Usually it's this zombie grunt. Every once in a while, though, I find a living soul who makes human-like conversation, and that's refreshing. But it's also few and far between. Sad to say, most people are just dead inside."

I was mulling this over when he joked, "For Halloween, I don't take my kids to a haunted house. I just bring them here to look at the zombies. My daughter still has nightmares from last year."

## You? Among The Living Dead?

So how would that airport worker describe *you* walking through the airport?

Not among the living dead I hope (later, I'll tell the story of how I almost got squashed at an airport...but I digress).

The identifiable characteristics of real-life zombies include a slouching walk, zero eye contact, obvious preoccupation, quick irritability and an absent, unchanging expression.

Ringing any bells here?

Once zombies find normal, flesh-and-blood humans, *they'll quickly feed off them.* And who can blame them? Zombies are absolutely starving for healthy, fulfilling lives.

*You say you don't like to refer to people as zombies?*

Fine. How about simply saying that "no one's at *The Helm?*"

# The "No One's At *The Helm*" Checklist:

What's life like when you're not at *The Helm*? Let's run through the checklist:

- For all intents and purposes, your ship is damaged and adrift—you have no real goals or dreams.

- Your ship turns sideways in rough seas instead of turning *into* the waves—in your effort to run from challenges rather than face them.

- Your ship capsizes at the first big wave—you quit, in other words, at the first sign of resistance.

- Your ship can't seem to break away from the reefs and rocky coast—you get derailed from your goals and dreams way too easily and are mired in negativity and self-pity._

- Your ship gets caught in flat seas—that's usually procrastination, an obsession with safety, and your inherent failure to take risks.

No offense, but if you checked even one of the above, chances are *no one's at YOUR Helm, either.*

If that's so, don't despair. It's why you're here.

You're here to change all that.

# Defining "Being At *The Helm*"

Alright, let's take another crack at this definition in one long sentence...

*To be at The Helm is to come to the realization that you are ultimately in 100% control of your life—no matter your circumstances, obstacles or tragedies—*

*and that, as long as you stay aware, you can choose the attitude and thoughts that will ultimately steer your life in a meaningful direction.*

## Excuse-Maker Machine

Notice I mentioned that circumstances were *not* an excuse?

Too often they are, though. How many times have you heard, "I would have (fill in the blank) if only (fill in the blank)"?

You can actually make a game of it. For example...

"I would have completed my degree, if only my roommate didn't secretly sell all my textbooks on www. SellAllMyTextbooks.com."

"I would have gotten my black belt, if only my Schitzu didn't eat my gi."

"I would have written that novel, if only I didn't keep dripping Hershey's Syrup on my keyboard."

"I would have gotten in terrific shape, if only I didn't start selling chili cheese dogs at the foodcourt."

*See how easy it is?*

The funniest thing about difficult circumstances is that they happen to all of us.

Every single one. No one's immune (despite what you might think). Trouble is one of the minimum requirements of this life; as if God, in His infinite wisdom, decided to toss challenges our way just to see how we'd react—to see whether we'd grow from them or head in full retreat.

Anybody can set sail in calm seas. You already know that. It's what happens in stormy seas that really defines who we are and what we're made of. Since everyone has daunting circumstances at one point or another—and since great men and women accomplish impressive things *anyway*—we must decide to set the "circumstance excuse" aside if we're ever to fulfill our tremendous potential.

## Circumstances Don't Make The Man Or Woman

Now, granted, horrendous things really *do* happen to people every day.

There are injuries to brains, spinal columns, legs, feet and hands. There are losses of parents, spouses, mentors and friends. We can be financially or legally nuked by one thing or another.

And sometimes these tragedies and incidents can *legitimately* cause us to alter our original plans.

But, that said, as tough as things can get, difficult circumstances simply aren't a good enough excuse for us *not* to fulfill our dreams.

James Allen, author of *"As a Man Thinketh,"* had this to say:

*"Circumstances don't make the man, they reveal him."*

Wow. Allen didn't think circumstances compromised us at all. Instead, he believed they put us center stage and revealed who we really are.

The same circumstances that can show one person to be strong and kind can expose another to be weak and mean.

*What do your circumstances reveal about you?*

*"A pessimist sees the difficulty in every opportunity; an optimist sees the opportunity in every difficulty."*

—Attributed to Winston Churchill—

## Surviving The Mind Pirates
## To Discover Troy

We already mentioned the zombies. But there's another threat we need to be on the lookout for as we gain control of our lives.

These are the mind pirates—negative *mateys* who take evil delight in crushing your initiatives, hopes and dreams.

Need an example? Alright...did you ever have a sudden flash of inspiration, an idea for promoting something new in an old way or making something old in a new way? Then make the mistake of mentioning it to someone... *only to have that person shoot your idea down as if he or she had some kind of cerebral machine gun?*

Say hello to the mind pirates.

The discovery of the fabled city of Troy from Homer's *Iliad* and the *Odyssey* came about only over the scorn of learned skeptics—mind pirates all who, in the "Age of Reasonableness" (following the "Age of Reason") were absolutely certain the city of Troy was just so much poetic imagery and never really existed at all.

They just knew that Heinrich Schliemann, the inspired explorer who ultimately uncovered Troy, was engaged in a wild goose chase.

Fortunately for us, Mr. Schliemann paid them no heed and discovered Troy anyway.

> *Mind pirates are skeptics, people with zero faith who can't create anything meaningful on their own or even see beyond the very next step. And since they can't see where they're going, they despise anyone who believes they can.*

Unfortunately, these skeptics rarely keep their opinions to themselves.

So here you go, minding your own business, which is all about this great "molecule" of an idea that just occurred to you. But your idea, at this conceptual stage, is weak, needs nurturing, and is entirely dependent on your continuing protection. It is, after all, at its most vulnerable point.

Now, coming at you from the other direction, is a mind pirate. He or she somehow senses you're carrying this molecule of an idea and, on instinct, instantly kicks into gear:

*"Oh, that will never work!"*

*"You'll lose everything!"*

*"You gotta be nuts!"*

*"C'mon, play it safe."*

*"Believe me, it'll put you back to square one."*

*"Think of your family."*

And on and on it goes. You've heard it all before, have undoubtedly been attacked by mind pirates at key moments in your life, right?

> **PRACTICAL TIP:** The first key to gaining control of your life is to shut these people out. Just like Heinrich Schliemann did. Don't listen to them. Don't give them any energy at all.
>
> Better yet, *don't share your "early" ideas with anyone except those you trust implicitly.* In this case anyway, keep your own counsel. Grab *The Helm* and steer clear

of these people whenever they appear. Protect your dreams from the mind pirates until they're big and strong enough to take care of themselves.

## Drop That Stick And Back Away...Now!

A few years ago a wealthy, sophisticated and very proper client, said "Doug, I can summarize your message in one little story..."

"My grandma lived on a ranch, was as tough as nails, and didn't beat around the bush. She had a way with words and always told me, 'In life, you have two choices: You can take control of your attitude or you can pick up the stick and stir the stink'n think'n!'"

I calmly asked, "Stir the stinking what?"

"The stink'n think'n. As a kid, Doug, didn't you ever come across something that, well, stunk to high heaven?"

"Sure. Every kid has," I said, quickly thumbing through my mental childhood files for everything from skunk cabbage to week-old roadkill.

"Right. And to make things worse, did you ever get a stick and start, you know, *poking it?*"

Said like that, it sounded pretty perverse. I admitted to doing it anyway. That kind of thing was probably standard for a kid.

"Right. Now when you stirred it, what did it do?"

"Stunk worse?"

"Exactly. It stunk worse."

I wasn't sure where this conversation was going.

"And, if you had any friends around, did you ever, well, *try flicking it onto them?* Be honest now."

What kid could resist the impulse of spreading something extremely gross to his nearest and dearest buddy?

"Guilty as charged."

## Misery Absolutely Loves Company

She continued: "We do that as adults, too. No, we don't go around flicking stinky stuff onto family members or anything like that. But we sure are experts at stirring the stink *in thinking*. You know what I mean. Looking around and seeing other people a lot happier than you—because your life isn't going all that well—you start stirring those rotten thoughts around in your brain. Insecurity, jealousy, inferiority, fear, feelings of not measuring up to those happy folks. Then what comes next?"

"Ahhh…"

"We flick these bad thoughts on them, right Doug?"

I started seeing her point.

## You? A Negativity Magnet?

There are people who, as soon as they roll out of bed, are hell-bent to flick that "stink" onto unsuspecting others. They actually go around searching for rotten stuff to tell everyone about. Call them the "Smell and Tell" folks.

"Did you hear the latest on the economy? Whoa!"

"Wonder what those terrorists are up to now?"

"What a corrupt bunch our politicians are."

*From there, they might make it a bit more personal, a bit more local.*

"If they'd only get out of my way around here, I'd do a great job."

"The boss is gonna run this company right into the ground. Wait and see."

"Are you as fed up with what they pay us as I am?"

You've heard it all before. Maybe you've even heard it today. *And maybe you were even the one stirring this kind of stink.*

What you're actually achieving when you spread this sort of toxic stuff around is making yourself a *negativity magnet.*

Negativity magnets attract all kinds of nasty stuff. Bad luck, bad grades, bad health, bad relationships. And, like the flu, the attitude is extremely contagious. You've probably found that, not wanting to catch this particular disease themselves, healthy folks will quickly evacuate your immediate vicinity whenever you're being negative and leave you quite alone, in much the same way they'd make themselves scarce if you were coughing and not covering your mouth.

Negativity can become a way of life, something you can grow quite comfortable with. But, tragically enough, you may only become aware of it after *you've wasted countless weeks, months and years becoming the very person you thought you despised.*

So how do you stop negativity dead in its tracks?

**PRACTICAL TIP:** The first step to stop this stink'n think'n thing is to become aware you're even doing it. And how do you do that? Well, one way is to count your negative thoughts.

That's right, count them.

For instance, on day one, you count your negative thoughts and come up with, maybe, 33 negative, stink-stirring thoughts. Okay, fine. The next day you count them and, because you're paying closer attention now, only come up with 18. The next day, still determined to change your attitude, you count just seven. The next day, just two. And the next day, maybe...*none*.

Does this really work? Yes...at least according to the editors of www.behavior.com. Here's their explanation: "Why could this work? Because you make yourself aware of obsessive thoughts in a *measurable way*. You associate it with a number, a number you're determined to lower. Turning it into this kind of simple, quantifiable task, *making almost a game of it*, can put the often daunting task of getting rid of obsessive thoughts well within your grasp."

*Growing aware of your thoughts is essential to your success. Once you gain that awareness and dry up those negative thoughts, you'll want to plant some good, supportive thoughts in their place.*

Okay, let's get back to the idea of grabbing *The Helm*. Here's one man's struggle.

## CASE HISTORY: How John B. Grabbed *The Helm* In The Middle Of A Storm

"My wife just filed for divorce, I've been sick for the past year—I feel pretty terrible right now, matter of fact—and the doctors have no idea what's happening. Tomorrow I'm scheduled to get an MRI to see what's going on. Because of all that, I'm missing a lot of work. I can't keep up and my performance is slipping. I don't even know if I can hang on to my job."

Those were the words of John B., a top business exec I happened to be coaching. He headed three divisions of this huge global organization, working seven days a week, putting in 12-18 hours a day. I asked him a simple question:

"Do you believe you're at *The Helm*?"

John looked at me like I was nuts.

"*The Helm*? Good luck with that. I'm down here stuck in the bilge."

Then he waxed surprisingly eloquent.

"It's funny. When you're not at *The Helm*, you lose yourself. You're no longer connected with life. I'm like a pinball, bouncing off one thing then another and with about as much control. Someone else has my *Helm*. I'm stuck below decks. *It's like someone else is charting my course through life!*"

Powerful words. And, yes, you're right, this did make John an official card-carrying zombie (yup, by law, zombies have to carry ID cards).

"My friend," I replied, "taking life by *The Helm* has literally become a matter of life or death for you now.

*"Often people attempt to live their lives backwards: they try to have more things, or more money, in order to do more of what they want so that they will be happier. The way it actually works is the reverse. You must first be who you really are, then, do what you need to do, in order to have what you want."*

—Margaret Young—

Your lack of control is making you sick. So what are you going to do about it?"

John looked around the room, finally focusing on his expensive Italian shoes. He answered, "Doug, I want to take *The Helm*...but I have no clue how to do it, no idea who I really am. I've lived like this for so long now, I'm not sure I can locate the real me. I hope I'm still in there someplace."

If you're like most people, you can relate at least on some level to John. Sometimes life has to go to the extreme before it gets your attention, just as it did with this top exec. John had to hit rock bottom before he woke up and could identify his biggest priorities. These turned out to be God, wife, family, health and then work, in that order.

---

**PRACTICAL TIP:** Are you heading for rock bottom just like John? Do you even know? Have you ever looked inside long enough to find out?

Alright, here's the tip: Go someplace nice and quiet. Leave the cell phones, the BlackBerries and the iPods at your desk. Get yourself comfortable and—ready for this now?—*do nothing for a half-hour.*

That's right. Absolutely nothing. At least outwardly. Inwardly, I want you to reflect on your life. Now maybe you haven't done this sort of thing before, so here's how it goes: Think of God and see what comes to mind; think of your family and see what comes to mind; think of your talents and see what comes to mind; think of what makes you happiest and see what comes to mind; think of what makes you unhappiest

> and see what comes to mind; think of your work and
> see what comes to mind.
>
> *Reflect.*

Take Socrates' advice: "The unexamined life is not worth living."

A word of warning here: This exercise can be a little uncomfortable if you've never examined your life before. Especially the do-nothing part. We're so used to multi-tasking and juggling a million things at once. But stick to it for the whole half-hour. You can even bring your watch, if you like, but don't keep checking it. Check inwardly instead.

For thirty minutes.

Why is this so important? Well, introspection practice is a valuable habit in improving your life, for one thing. Call it "course correction." Call it whatever you like. But it's you saying, "I'm not going to let life just happen to me—I'm going to do my deliberate best to *direct* my life."

Just sit quietly for a half-hour.

This is important because it's always a smart idea to see where you are before grabbing *The Helm* and steering to someplace new. I invite you to do this monthly, and I promise some useful good will come of it.

Happily, and after some of this reflection, John B. woke up. He examined his life, saw what made him happiest, what made him unhappiest, grabbed *The Helm* and charted a brand-new course.

His health improved, his happiness soared, and he was able to repair those family relationships that were most important to him. Again, the strange thing here was that John didn't even realize he had hit bottom, and if you had asked him whether or not he was growing as a human being, he probably would have given you an enthusiastic thumbs up.

But he was asleep back then, busy with matters he thought were important but really weren't, working his tail off and heading exactly in the wrong direction. His journey to grab *The Helm* started with one small decision. Not ten or fifteen.

One.

*You are literally one decision away from revolutionizing your life.*

One decision away from escaping the zombies and mind pirates in your life.

## What's It Like Being At *The Helm*?

We've talked about some important things in this chapter, including the zombies...the mind pirates... the stink stirrers...how circumstances don't make the man...the value of keeping your goals and dreams close to your vest...avoiding Socrates' "unexamined life" syndrome by sitting quietly for a half-hour...and the "No One's At *The Helm*" Checklist.

Let's conclude the chapter with another checklist. This one is the "What's It Like Being At *The Helm*" checklist. Here goes...

- You have a direction—you're on course, feel optimistic and are ready to arrive.

- You face every oncoming wave *head on*.

- You don't capsize, no matter how big the wave. You keep working, keep problem-solving, and keep doing whatever it takes to stay on course.

- You steer clear of rocks and reefs. You stay on the lookout for dangers, but put your energy into finding smoother routes (rather than trying to push rocks out of your way). Your eyes are straight ahead and just a little further down the road (you've noticed how, when driving a car, you can't look to the side for very long before drifting in that direction). Similarly, when at *The Helm*, troubling people who appear in your life—like jagged rocks— are given little energy or focus. Your focus is on your journey, not their rough edges. You escape the rocks and reef precisely by *not* making them your focus.

- You don't flounder. You know where you're headed and what you're doing.

- You seize opportunities and are prepared to sail full speed ahead when the wind shows up. And when there's no wind, *you row*.

*"No matter what problem you may have
to face today, there is a solution, because
you have nothing to deal with but your own
thoughts. As you know, you have the power
to select and control your thoughts, difficult
though it may be at times to do so. As long
as you think that your destiny is in the hands
of other people, the situation is hopeless.*

*Remind yourself constantly that you have
nothing to deal with but your own thoughts.
Write this down where you will see it often.
Have it on your desk. Hang it in your
bedroom. Write it in your pocketbook.
Write it on your soul."*

—Emmett Fox—

# Chapter 3

# DON'T SINK YOURSELF!

We talked about zombies, mind pirates and stink stirrers, and why you should avoid these kinds of people—*or avoid becoming these kinds of people*—at all costs as you make your way to *The Helm*.

But these three only represent *external threats* to you gaining control over your life.

What about the *internal ones?*

Are you sabotaging your own efforts to improve yourself? That's the real question, of course. And it's exactly what can keep you adrift in the fog for years to come if you don't watch out.

## What Happens When You Don't Keep Watch

Heard the one about the frog in a pan of water on a stove?

You probably have. There's this frog in a cool pan of water on the stove. How'd it get there? Not important. Maybe someone was desperately hungry and went frog-hunting. Maybe the dumb frog broke into the home and thought a pan on the stove was a good place to be. Who knows?

Anyway, the burner temperature is slowly turned up by some sinister someone. Click by sinister click.

We're supposed to believe that this particular frog remains keenly unaware of those *slight increases* in heat. Maybe it even enjoys the warmth.

Until it's too late. The dumb frog stays put long enough to become the evening meal.

So...in real life, could you literally cook a frog this way? Probably not (although the analogy had to come from someplace, right?). But the point is well made.

*Because the indignities of an unfulfilled life can mount slowly, even tolerably (and maybe even comfortably), we are often blissfully unaware of just how very far off course we actually are until it's too late.*

It's a process I earnestly hope is not happening to you.

## Poof...Your Dreams Vanish

It's all about illusions. *Your* mental illusions.

Chances are, you've seen David Copperfield, Lance Burton or some other world-class magician do their act, right? If not, invest a little time watching one. It's very instructive to see a state-of-the-art illusionist in action. What the right hand is doing...what the left hand is doing...what you're made to see...what you're not made to see.

How far from reality it all is.

Make no mistake, illusions, for entertainment purposes, are wonderful things. But there's nothing funny about the cerebral illusions we foist on ourselves.

Remember John B. in the last chapter? The top executive who deluded himself into believing he was living the good life? *All mental illusion.*

A mental illusion that wasted a great deal of the man's life.

And that could be your problem, too. Over our lives, we can build entire illusions around a sliver of truth. We can construct veritable mansions of self-deception, complete with wings of exaggeration, upper floors of fake satisfaction, basements of "it's really not that bad."

Yes, entire estates of illusion can actually occupy your time and eventually, over the course of a lifetime, mask your realities and the things that could otherwise bring you the happiest moments of your life.

If you're not aware.

## The Matrix Of Your Life

Did you happen to catch any of *The Matrix* movies?

The first of the three starts out with Neo, your typical computer programmer, who believes he's living a normal, if monumentally empty life in 1999. But he's a loner who can't seem to sleep, can't seem to find the source of his emptiness...until somebody (by the name of Trinity) drops by.

Now without spoiling the plot of the movie, in the event you were lost in a Brazilian jungle the year the movie came out and haven't seen it yet, Trinity reveals to Neo the *actual* reality of his life. And it's profoundly, *elaborately* different from the paltry life Neo *thinks* he's living.

Not that this new reality is any paradise. Great risks, dangers and challenges abound.

But at least Neo knows the truth now, the purpose of his life, the great potential lying ahead of him, and the satisfaction of helping others with the skills and powers he possesses.

And that's a lot more satisfying than the previous mind-numbing life he believed he was living.

## So, Your First Step: Awareness

As in *The Matrix*, where Neo had *zero* awareness of his real situation at the start, awareness is your challenge here, too.

Okay...so how do you become aware of *your own* mental illusions?

PRACTICAL TIP: Even if you've seen The Matrix already, watch it again. Pay close attention to the elaborate illusions everyday people had constructed. See the tremendous difference between what people *thought* they were doing and what was *actually* happening.

Now, granted, this is only a movie. But, as mentioned in the previous chapter, do some reflection about it.

Go to your favorite place, sit quietly for a half-hour and think about the potential illusions you've fostered in your life, what actually might be your present-day reality, and, most importantly, how you can have your very own "Trinity moment."

Your job at this moment is to get to *ground level* in your life, the place where there's no more fantasy or fallacy, just bottom-line truth—the truth about you, your skills and talents, your weaknesses and shortcomings.

*You.*

It's time to start leaving your illusions behind.

## The Reincarnation Lesson

Like me, you don't have to believe in reincarnation to learn something important from it (along the lines of what we're now talking about).

If you've ever listened to people tell stories about their past lives, you might detect a common thread: A disproportionate number of these folks insist they've lived past lives of *great meaning and grandeur.*

"Yeah, this may sound funny, but I was a king in the Middle Ages"..."I was a lady in Buckingham Palace"..."I discovered fire"..."I discovered cashmere"..."I directed the building of a pyramid"..."I was Daniel Boone at the Alamo"..."I helped invent penicillin."

You get the idea. Few people who believe in reincarnation like to think of themselves as being a *nobody* in a *nothing* life (in the movie, *Defending Your Life,* there's a hilarious scene about this very thing—I recommend you seeing it).

You never hear: "I barely eked out a living as a serf for a king in the Middle Ages"..."I lived in boxcars most of my life"..."I slipped on a banana peel trying to make my way to the Alamo"... "I was one of the many workers who tripped and fell off the top of the pyramid"..."Three people knew my name before I got eaten by that lion."

Ever wonder why that is (apart from the possibility that some folks really did live past lives of grandeur)? It's likely because, down deep inside, *we believe in ourselves*, in our abilities to "right the ship" and enjoy our own version of greatness.

We never think of ourselves as being nothing or of not figuring things out before we die.

The hopeless romantic inside each of us believes we'll have a happy ending.

And that's actually a wonderful thing. It means we understand, at least on some level, that we have the potential for greatness inside us.

*It means we have the highest hopes for ourselves.*

But it also means we have an equally large capacity for illusion and self-deception. That's not a commentary on reincarnation, mind you, but on our almost infinite ability to see ourselves in an unrealistic light.

*"The ingenuity of self-deception is inexhaustible."*

—Hannah Moore—

## Disabling Your Negative Filter

Remember "stirring the stink" from the last chapter? How could you forget, right?

Well, as mentioned, if you entertain too much negativity, *that becomes your reality*. Your self-deception, you could say. Surrounding you. From morning until night.

In psychology, we call this the "negative filter." It refers to a cognitive distortion in which someone literally *distorts their world* based on their own negative thinking. Everything that passes through that person's senses goes through this negative filter before being allowed to enter the brain.

For example, let's say someone did you a nice, little favor—and you had a negative filter installed—you might think:

"What's this guy really up to?"

"Probably trying to gain my trust so he can steal from me down the road."

"Bet he's doing this because he feels sorry for me."

"What a show-off."

"So I got some help. So what? I'm so far behind, I'll never catch up."

Instead of expressing your gratitude for the kindness, in other words, you turn everything inward. The moment centers on you and your insecurities.

*See how negativity can distort your reality?*

If you always run every single detail of your life through this negative filter, then you'll end up excluding the positive, will always be suspicious of motives, and lack enough faith for good outcomes. This can give you an inaccurate view of the world and saddle you with poor performance and unnecessary failure.

In life, there's always a balance between the negative and the positive. It's not all one-way.

*"The greatest discovery of my generation is that man can alter his life simply by altering his attitude of mind."*

—Attributed to William James—

## Too Much Negativity And
## You Become A Skeptic

What's more, with this negative filter firmly in place, you run the risk of becoming a full-blown skeptic.

As mentioned earlier, a skeptic is usually a huge fan of the status quo and has very little faith left in his or her tank to try something new. Moreover, skeptics avoid risk and are instantly suspicious of anyone who doesn't.

As historian and essayist Thomas Carlyle put it, "Skepticism...is not intellectual only; it is moral also; a chronic atrophy and disease of the whole soul. A man lives by believing something; not by debating and arguing many things."

Skeptics could also be called *anti-creative*. "In and of itself, skepticism has made no actual contribution to science," wrote Deepak Chopra, "just as music reviews in the newspaper make no contribution to the art of composition and book reviewing falls far short of writing books."

*How true! Far easier to be a critic of the creative work someone else has labored long and hard to complete rather than undertake such a monumental work yourself.*

Ever check with a critic before going to a movie? It took a veritable army of creative people working for months on end under tight budgets and tighter deadlines to complete that film...yet a relative few minutes for a critic to casually dispense his or her all-important opinion of the movie's relative merits.

Doesn't seem quite fair, does it?

I've always found it better just to go to a movie and form my own opinion anyway.

## Cynicism—Another Charming
## Quality Of The Stink Stirrer

*"A cynic is a man who, when he smells flowers, looks around for a coffin."* So wrote Henry Louis Mencken.

Another fruit of a 24/7 negative filter is cynicism.

*www.dictionary.com* defines the word as *"a person who believes that only selfishness motivates human actions and who disbelieves in or minimizes selfless acts."*

Talk about your negativity taking over!

Here's a news flash: **Human beings are entirely capable of selfless acts!** Random acts of kindness take place all the time. You have only to recall the tragic crash of Air Florida flight 90 into the Potomac back in 1982.

When a rescue helicopter arrived and lowered a line to the six survivors of that flight in the ice-cold Potomac, Arland Dean Williams Jr. repeatedly passed it onto others. Every time the line came back to him, he passed it to someone else, someone he didn't know. And all the while he must have been in the kind of great pain cold causes.

Williams kept doing that until he sank below the frigid waters.

Need to read a few more of these inspiring stories? There are several Websites, such as *www.actsofkindness.org*, devoted to recording selfless acts of kindness, but cynicism can assign dark motives to virtually every kindness.

## Looping Negativity

Too much pessimism can simply immobilize you.

Granted, there's something useful called "defensive pessimism. "That's when you look a situation up one side and down the other, identifying all the possible things that can go wrong, then design a strategy to deal with those risks.

That kind of risk management is just a smart part of any successful planning.

But it's when you identify all the risks, *yet never give yourself the go-ahead to proceed* that lands you squarely in the pessimist's camp.

You've heard of music being "looped," of making a particular sequence of music repeat over and over again? Well, the pessimist's mind is looped as well, but to repeatedly find everything wrong with a situation.

And it's that kind of looped behavior that results in absolutely nothing constructive ever happening.

Ever.

## Paralyzed By Fear

Then there's pessimism's first cousin, fear.

The classic extremes, in the investment world at least, are fear on one end of the scale and greed on the other. We hear all the time of investors who greedily fall for get-rich-quick Ponzi schemes and the panic that later sets in when the pitiful truth emerges and these folks fear they'll lose all their money. Witness the monstrous Bernie Madoff con game.

Sure, we don't come across extremes like that every day. Most of us don't fall for get-rich-quick schemes, so most of us don't get scared to death over losing our money. Still, we pretty much all find ourselves somewhere on the greed/fear scale. We want the rewards in life—often extremely generous rewards, too—but the fear is never very far away.

Remember the mind pirates? Fear is like having a mind pirate stuck *inside your brain* pretty much repeating those same old things:

*"Oh, that will never work!"*

*"You'll lose everything!"*

*"You gotta be nuts!"*

*"C'mon, play it safe."*

*"Believe me, this'll put you right back to square one."*

*"Think of your family."*

It's easy for this kind of risk-aversion to take root in your heart, especially if you work in a corporate hierarchy. In this kind of atmosphere where everyone is always watching everyone else, there's a tendency for employees to play it safe and stick to the status quo.

## Fear As A Case Study

I recently worked with a senior VP who actually was, himself, a buttoned-down version of fear.

Sure, the man appeared strong and determined, yet beneath the tough exterior he had become a corporate coward and a shell of what he used to be. Remember the pilot in the movie *Top Gun* who lost his nerve and had to wash out of the program? Well, this was my client's problem.

Except he didn't wash out of the program. He stayed hidden in corporate camouflage and played it safe with every decision.

He only played defense. Never offense.

My client would only agree to assignments he knew he could control. He shied away from new challenges that could leave him vulnerable or force him to deal with uncertainty. As a result, his division struggled due to a lack of real leadership, courage, innovation and clear direction.

He confided in me that...

"I feel like a scared little boy afraid to make a mistake and disappoint daddy, which was, of course, the CEO. I'm embarrassed to admit this, but often, when I get a great idea I think can really help, I'll quickly dismiss it because, simply put, I might fail to execute it. Either that or someone else might think it's just plain dumb."

"I once had an idea to take our product into a new market, but *fear* said it would never work. So I said nothing. Two weeks later, a colleague shared the very same idea in a senior management meeting, and it was a big hit!"

So who do *you* consult when making your decisions?

*Fear?*

## Some Words Of Advice From FDR

Fear will always give you an answer 180 degrees from your true potential. *Always!*

As kids we sure didn't rely on fear, did we? Think back to those days. We were liberated, spirited and free-wheeling back then. If you ever brought up all the things that could go wrong as a kid, your buddies would quickly yell, "Fraidy cat! Fraidy cat!"

Along those lines, most folks remember Franklin Delano Roosevelt's majestic words at his Inaugural Address in the midst of the Great Depression:

*"The only thing we have to fear is fear itself."*

But it's what he said next that really hits home.

*"...nameless, unreasoning, unjustified terror which paralyzes needed efforts to convert retreat into advance."*

Wow. *"...which paralyzes needed efforts to convert retreat into advance."* Aren't those amazing words? Don't they just hit the nail right on the head?

Does your fear paralyze you into retreating when you should be advancing?

As said, defensive pessimism—or defensive fear—plays a key role in good decision-making. But irrational fear spilling out of every orifice of your body only ensures you'll experience the same old failure you've been experiencing all along.

Want to know the *scariest* part of consulting fear to make your decisions? The scariest part is that the people and organizations governed by fear are often unaware that fear governs them.

*They're not aware of what they are not aware of.*

And that's *their* mental illusion.

## The Courage To, Yes, Take Courage

*"To see what is right, and not to do it,
is want of courage."*

—Confucius—

Good old Confucius. What a wise old guy. He certainly nailed that one on the head.

My client in the above section knew he had a great corporate solution, but simply failed to act.

He lacked courage, plain and simple.

So what if he had acted on his idea? Then he would have enjoyed the "homerun" his colleague enjoyed instead. He would have gained confidence in his ideas and how he employed his courage and would have busted out of his fear cycle.

He would have made some major progress in his life, in other words.

This one simple idea can revolutionize your life: *Consult courage when making decisions in your life. Not fear.*

Sure, even with courage, you'll fail at times. We all do. But failure isn't nearly as bad as we make it out to be. As humans we pretend to be perfect and detest failure. But learning from failure can be one of the most powerful ways we learn, our foundation for improvement.

*If* we take courage.

## Breaking Your Courage Down To The Molecular Level

Writing in *The Journal of Positive Psychology*, Colonel Sean Hannah and his colleagues at the United States Military Academy, offer a new and specific model of courage. Their model includes traits, states of mind and convictions. Let's first look at...

## Courageous Character Traits

Traits are a distinguishing characteristic or quality, something not likely to budge or give way very easily. Here are the traits that contribute to courage...

1) **Openness to experience:** This trait is about being open to trying new things. Openness is an important part of courage.

*"The bravest thing you can do when you are not brave is to profess courage and act accordingly."*

—Corra Harris—

2) **Conscientiousness:** These are the dependable folks *who feel a sense of duty towards themselves and others.* Because of that, they get the job done. How can you increase your conscientiousness? Voluntarily shouldering responsibility is one way (which is probably why conscientiousness increases with age).

3) **Core Self-Evaluation:** Remember that half-hour of quiet reflection we talked about? An honest review of your outlook on life, assessing your strengths and weaknesses, can contribute to *a feeling of control* over situations.

## Courageous States Of Mind

A state of mind is what's occupying that old cranium of yours at any given moment. The states of mind that enable courage include...

1) **Self-Efficacy:** This essentially means confidence in yourself and your ability to provide effective solutions for present-day challenges.

2) **Means Efficacy:** Simply put, this refers to the inner tools you believe are available for you to get the job done.

3) **State Hope:** Somewhere inside, you have to believe that accomplishing the task *is entirely possible,* before you figure out a way to go about it.

4) **Resilience:** This is your "bounce-back-ability." It's also about maintaining the belief that you will overcome the situation, come what may.

Can you increase your resilience? Research suggests expressing positive emotions may do that. "Generating amusement, interest or any other positive emotion is likely to increase levels of resilience. Essentially, it may be possible to laugh off the fear often experienced when being courageous," wrote Hannah.

## Convictions And Social Forces

The last parts of Hannah and his colleagues' model of courage include...

1) **Inner Convictions:** You can describe these convictions in one word: *Nobility*. Noble attributes include independence, selflessness, integrity and honor...exactly the kind of beliefs that crush fear.

2) **Social Forces:** Let's face it, seeing how others react to a situation is key to the way we react ourselves. The cowardly person sees the crowd's reaction and adopts it as their own. The courageous person sees the crowd's reaction and wonders how he or she can *help or help lead* the crowd.

Interesting study. Hope you get something out of it.

You were made to live a courageous life and not hold on to your safety blanket like little Linus in Peanuts. In fact, courage is one of the minimum requirements of Taking Life by The Helm.

**PRACTICAL TIP:** Okay, enough theory. Think of this as your "courage exercise." Sometime during the coming day or so, take courage and *make yourself* speak up about something.

You could speak up and introduce yourself to someone new. You could speak up and offer an idea at a work meeting (where you'd otherwise stay quiet).

You could speak up at church, a PTA meeting, a get-together of friends.

Whatever the venue, *speak up!* Force yourself, if you have to. Say something helpful and/or intelligent.

Just like you'd pump iron to build your biceps or ride your bike to build endurance, speaking up when it really isn't all that comfortable to do so will help build your "courage muscles."

## Perfection Is Not The Name Of The Game—Learning From Your Mistakes Is

Some leaders and parents create cultures that do not tolerate mistakes.

And, in so doing, they preclude the possibility that their followers or kids will learn from their mistakes…which, as just mentioned, *is one of the top ways we human beings learn!*

We're not designed to be perfect, yet we often pretend to be. What a recipe for stress! Pretending to be perfect (when you and your organization are clearly not) leads to fear, blame, excuses and rationalizations.

Stink stirring, in other words.

## To Summarize…

This chapter is about ways you can inadvertently sabotage yourself. Are there other ways to scuttle your ship? Of course, they're limited only by your imagination. But this will at least get you thinking.

*"Don't be a cynic and disconsolate preacher. Don't bewail and moan. Omit the negative propositions. Challenge us with incessant affirmatives. Don't waste yourself in rejection, or bark against the bad, but chant the beauty of the good."*

—Ralph Waldo Emerson—

As you read on, page by page, I hope you see the importance of growing more aware of yourself, of the negative things you sometimes do, and what you can do to stay positive and on course.

And I hope you see the dangers of mental illusions, of being self-deluded, and of being a "deer in the headlights" from all the fear, both inside and outside your world.

In the next chapter, we'll work on increasing your awareness so you can become even more aware of where you are and where you want to be.

*"He who knows not, and knows not that he knows not, is a fool; shun him. He who knows not, and knows that he knows not, can be taught; teach him. He who knows, and knows not that he knows, is asleep; wake him. He who knows, and knows that he knows, is a prophet; follow him."*

—Persian apothegm—

# Chapter 4

# PEELING OFF THE LABELS

## *Becoming aware of what you don't know you don't know!*

I was walking behind two people at a mall and, okay, I admit it, I was eavesdropping. This is what I overheard:

> *"I loved you in that dress. Doesn't matter that it's a plus size. You're a great-looking plus size. Always will be."*

Now I know this person was just trying to be kind to her friend, but what was she really saying here?

*She was telling her friend that she believed she'd always be an overweight gal.*

That's what her words boiled down to when she threw out that inadvertent compliment. It was as if she were sticking a specific and unflattering label on her friend.

And her friend was probably only too content to let her do just that.

## Peeling The Labels Off Our Lives

Have some of your loved ones also stuck a label on you that, like this overweight gal, you weren't consciously aware of and have been inadvertently wearing all these years?

Well? Have you been labeled?

No matter who did the labeling, such a thing can alter the way you view your world. A client recently related the following story (it's been changed to protect her identity).

"We were picking teams for soccer. Only this time Chad, the team captain, whose team I was supposed to be on, said, 'We don't want you on our side. Man, you're so fat and slow. Just sit over there and watch.'"

"Inside, I was crying, I was so embarrassed. I couldn't believe he just said that to me in front of all my classmates. I wanted to tackle him and sit on him until he popped. I couldn't hold my hurt in any longer and cried my eyes out all the way home."

"My mom noticed and asked, 'What's wrong, dear?'"

"'They made fun of me at school, said I was fat and slow, and didn't want me on their team. No one likes me.'"

## That's When Her Mom Whipped Out A Brand-New Label

"'Oh honey, I'm so sorry,' she said. 'I feel so bad for you. But maybe it's time you faced facts.'"

"'You're a heavy girl, sweetheart. I'm sad to say that you're fat, just like your mom. There'll be some things in life you simply won't be able to do. The truth is—and I know this is hard—but you'll probably never be popular or have lots of friends. At least, though, you'll always have me.'"

*Ouch!*

"I believed everything my mom told me as though it were the gospel truth! For *twenty long years*, I willingly kept that label on myself. For *twenty long years*, I believed it was the truth. For *twenty long years*, that's how I saw myself—believing I wasn't good enough and couldn't measure up. Everything I looked at was tainted by the label my mom and classmates stuck on me that horrible day!"

It took my soccer-playing client twenty infinitely long years before she got to the point of questioning this label. After some painful self-examination, she finally realized *she didn't have to believe everything her mom or classmates or anyone else told her about herself.*

Ever. She was the expert on herself. *Period.*

Was there some truth to her being heavy on *that particular day twenty years ago?* Yes. She *was* heavy at that moment. But by sticking a "big, fat and slow" label on her that day, her mom and classmates overlooked the fact that we're all human beings in a kind of dynamic transition.

## New Cells, Every New Day

For one thing, it's calculated that your cells are capable of effectively replacing themselves on the order of about once a year.

That means the "you" of last year—or twenty years ago, for that matter—is long gone and has literally been replaced by a brand-new you.

You're constantly changing whether you realize it or not. Or believe it or not.

So if someone stuck a label on you twenty years ago, it is absolutely, positively obsolete by now. You're a whole new person. Literally.

You were actually a whole new person not long after the label first stuck, though you didn't know it at the time.

## You're Changing As You Read This!

What am I getting at? Not only are people capable of change, *we're undergoing change right this very second.*

Sure, some of that change is biological, as I just mentioned, with the incredible turnover of cells.

But it goes deeper than that.

You're reading this book, aren't you? And why? Because you're now at the point in life when you're ready to make a change, to improve in possibly dramatic fashion. Maybe it took you several days to arrive at this moment in time. Maybe several months or years.

*Maybe even a whole lifetime.*

And over that time, you may have been taking baby steps toward this very second, toward consciously wanting to change for the better. Maybe you didn't even notice those baby steps.

But whether you did or not, important change was occurring.

## Einstein's Fifteen-Minute-A-Day Change Habit

What am I leading up to?

Just this: Your thinking, on any given day, at any given moment, governs who you are. Grow aware of the labels in your life, and you can instantly begin peeling them off.

*Instantly!*

So how, exactly? By first deciding what kind of human being you want to be.

You say you'd love to see what it's like to live your life maybe 50 pounds lighter? Or as a pilot? Or as a radio talk show host?

Or as the driver of a Zamboni machine (a Zamboni machine, for the uninitiated, is that streetsweeper-like vehicle that drives around hockey rinks, between periods, grooming the ice)?

Wherever your interest lies, *make that your focus.* Don't misunderstand, I'm not saying to engage in the same kind of lame cross-your-fingers, wishful thinking that a lot of today's self-help gurus want to teach you.

I'm a lot more "real-world practical" than that.

What I am saying is that you *work* toward your goal a little bit each day.

As in fifteen-minute segments.

---

**PRACTICAL TIP:** According to *www.behavior.com*, Albert Einstein had this wonderful piece of advice about the power of learning something a bit at a time: "Anyone can be a genius if they pick one specific subject and study it diligently just 15 minutes each day for a year."

*Anyone can be a genius...if they pick one specific subject...and study it diligently just 15 minutes each day for a year.*

---

*Wow. How neat is that?* Do *you* have 15 minutes a
day? Would *you* like to be a genius at something? How
about a genius at losing weight? Or at communicating
better with strangers, friends or groups?

Or at driving that cool Zamboni machine?

There's no law that says you have to attend a
university to learn something, you know. Learning
doesn't always have to come through official channels
with credits, degrees or career motivations. It's okay
to learn something *just because you want to.*

*This 15-minute-a-day plan of Einstein's could be
just what you need to change your life at a very
comfortable pace.*

## So What Happened To
## My Soccer-Playing Client?

It was only after my client took ownership of her feelings
as an adult that she could finally take *The Helm*, refute
those nasty young adult illusions, and replace them
with a confident, optimistic plan.

Here's what she had to say after ripping those self-
limiting labels off:

"I finally asked myself, is this why I am alive? To feel
like crap? Or is there more to this life? Is there more for
me? Deep down, I believed there was. God had given me
talents and skills. I didn't know what they were just yet.
It's hard to find room to focus on anything else when
your obsession is yourself and all the things you aren't."

"I now know that my life has more to do with what I give than what I take. That's what makes me beautiful." With tears in her eyes she added, "And I am beautiful."

And she is.

"I get it now. I'm aware now. I threw all those old labels and limitations away. Now the coolest thing is, I'm the team captain of an indoor soccer team and loving every minute of it. *The team captain!* I wonder how many of my old classmates are still playing and enjoying soccer? I'm also a den mother and my little Cub Scouts love me. On top of it all, I'm married to a wonderful man who loves me very much."

"Sure the labels others stick on us hurt...but not nearly as much as the labels we apply to ourselves."

I'm not ashamed to say I wiped tears of joy from my eyes as I sat and watched her escape her self-imposed prison. It was truly a moving experience to witness and the reason I'm in this business.

*Nothing touches me more than seeing someone resolve, in the marrow of their soul, to become unstoppable in doing those things that used to seem impossible!*

That same spirit of hers to take *The Helm* is inside you too...no matter how gloomy life may now look or tired you may now feel.

## The Selfishness Of Inferiority

This brings up a good point: *Not feeling good about yourself can be a very selfish pastime.*

Huh?

It's absolutely true. Just like my client who was preoccupied with her own sense of inferiority, you can spend an unbelievable amount of time concerned with

*"Anybody can be great, because anybody can serve."*

—Martin Luther King Jr.—

yourself, with what people think of you, the way you look, how you act or the kind of impression you're making.

And, all the while, that time could be better spent in much more satisfying, more beneficial pursuits.

Like helping others.

How many nights, for example, have you stayed home because you didn't feel good about yourself? Or didn't have the right clothes, haircut or belt size?

Put another way, because you've been so preoccupied with yourself (if this is, in fact, the case), you've essentially *robbed* yourself of an opportunity to get out, interact, and possibly help others in *their* time of need.

Like I said, inferiority can be very selfish.

## Helper's High: What Is It And Where To Get It

It's not as if helping others is a dreary, thankless chore, you know...something you have to drag yourself out the front door to do.

The fact is, for some people, *it can be kind of a high.*

"Helper's High," to be specific. This is the term applied to the good feelings people often get when they help others. Quoting from a story on a study by Dr. Allen Luks...

"Dr. Luks studied 3,000 volunteers of all ages at more than 20 organizations throughout the country to see if there was a correlation between acts of kindness and good physical and mental health."

"Apparently, there was. The gracious volunteers in Luks' study testified to feeling a rush of euphoria following an act of kindness. That led to a prolonged period of calm— Luks' 'Helper's High.' This included a sharp reduction in stress and the apparent release of the body's natural painkillers, the endorphins."

"According to Dr. Luks, the initial rush generated by acts of kindness or generosity is followed by a longer-lasting period of improved emotional well-being. 'Helping contributes to the maintenance of good health, and it can diminish the effect of diseases and disorders, both serious and minor, psychological and physical,' Dr. Luks concluded."

"So if you'd like to feel good inside, why not put Dr. Luks' findings to the test and volunteer to help someone? Might be just the thing to take the bite out of today's headlines."

To that I lend my whole-hearted support.

## Awareness Is The First Step
## To Doing Something Different

As mentioned, your first step is to become aware that there even is a problem.

What's more, you need to realize that the solution ultimately resides in *your thinking*. My client came to grips with her problem and ultimately told herself that it was okay to play soccer even as a mom, notwithstanding all the negative labels that she and others had placed on her.

What took her so long? She couldn't blame her "barometers"—her feelings. They were working just fine. They told her things weren't going so well...but she had long ago numbed herself to that kind of feedback.

She simply refused to receive the messages her feelings were trying to send her.

It's like her emotions were texting her, but she never turned her phone on long enough to receive the messages.

It all begins with awareness.

So if you aren't feeling the level of peace you'd like, go do some honest reflection. Don't take 20 years to realize you're off course.

You can begin *today* to liberate yourself from those nasty mental illusions!

## The Childhood Sponge

When you were a child, you were like a sponge soaking up suggestions.

Unfortunately, if you were like most kids, a great many of those early suggestions were negative, setting us on a rocky course right off the bat. As a mature adult, though, you now can challenge and replace those mental illusions any time you want.

What signals you that you have, in fact, replaced those illusions with truth?

*Peace.* You'll enjoy a deep sense of peace.

Keep this in mind, though: Peace is not necessarily the "easy way out." I'm sure, on some level, Martin Luther King Jr. would rather have avoided the national spotlight in order to live a "normal" life...but that wouldn't have brought peace to his soul.

In Native American wisdom, "A warrior would rather die in defeat than to go against his nature."

Peace isn't always so peaceful.

## Only Two

Here's something else to be aware of: There really are only two major emotions.

*Love and fear.*

All the others stem from these two. Many folks report that nearly two-thirds of their thinking is based on

"What will happen will happen whether you are afraid or not. Go forward with a brave heart, trusting God."

—Doug Nielsen—

fear and negativity...which means, if this is the case with you, that *only a third* of your brain and heart is positively "operating" your life.

So what percentage of *your* thinking is negative? Do your fears have an undue influence on your life? Fears... such as...

- Fear of rejection

- Fear of success

- Fear that you don't measure up

- Fear of making the wrong decision

- Fear of letting go and not being in control

- Fear of the unknown and uncertainty

- Fear of losing everything

- Fear of trusting others or systems

- Fear of what others think of you

- Fear that you'll never achieve peace

- Fear of only being as good as your last success

This certainly isn't a complete list. Fear comes in all sizes and shapes. Maybe there's a fear not listed here that you know only too well.

And maybe you understand how fear builds on itself and tends to flow downhill without direction. If that's the case, it might help you to understand why bad things can and sometimes do happen in your life.

"How come things never go my way? How come I'm always left out? How come I feel so numb?"

The answer is as ancient as the Bible: *You sow what you reap!*

So the question you need to be asking yourself is, *what do I keep sowing?*

Not just you, but your job and sometimes your company's culture can be a reflection of your negative thoughts. After all, the difference between you and your competitors boils down to thinking, learning and executing, doesn't it?

If you and your team are negative thinkers, you put your company at a distinct disadvantage from day one.

## Your Own Forbidden Planet

There's a great old sci-fi flick called *Forbidden Planet.*

In it, a crew from Earth lands on this mysterious planet with only a couple of occupants: a scientist and his beautiful daughter (played by Anne Francis).

Almost immediately a gigantic, unseen monster begins attacking the crew (led by Leslie Nielsen—yeah, he was a serious actor before he became a comedian).

Turns out the scientist (Walter Pidgeon) had been using this incredibly powerful technology a former race of aliens had left behind. What did the technology do?

*It magnified and manifested the thoughts of anyone using it.*

So, without realizing what he was doing, the scientist had been transforming his fears and resentments over the crew's mission—to take the two back to Earth— into a real-life monster capable of preventing that from happening.

When he finally figured it out, he was able to stop this seemingly indestructible beast *by simply changing his thoughts.*

Question: What are your thoughts turning into at work? Or at home?

A monster?

Or something heroic?

## Not Just The Way It Is

The *emotional* nature of an organization is connected with its level of performance (see Daniel Goleman's research at www.danielgoleman.info).

It's true. A team's morale can either be fear-based or love-based.

If fear-based, illusions can stymie the team's potential.

If love-based, the sky's the limit.

As a leader, it's important to be aware of the emotional tenor of your group and to challenge the "that's just the way it is" environment.

*Don't let any one person determine the emotional threshold of your team.*

Ask yourself if your corporate culture is creating a foundation that can unleash the human spirit of greatness.

Or something far short.

Now let's see how we can become better decision-makers.

*"Man is programmed to find
the programmer."*

—Kedar Joshi—

# Chapter 5

# CHOOSING TO MAKE GOOD DECISIONS

## *Being nudged by your north star.*

In Chapter 3, you learned about your inner adversaries. You learned that your thinking is ultimately responsible for your feelings, and if your thinking is distorted, *ditto for your feelings.*

The key to seeing things as they really are is your *North Star*. You need to learn if your thoughts are in sync with it.

Your *North Star*...what is the symbolism here?

According to *www.wikipedia.com*, "The North Star has historically been used for navigation, both to find the direction of north and to determine latitude. It always appears due north in the sky, and the angle it makes with respect to the horizon is equal to the latitude of the observer. The North Star is visible only in northern hemisphere skies and so cannot be used for navigation south of the equator."

So...the North Star has always been a constant to mariners looking to navigate north of the equator. Similarly, in our case, I refer to the *North Star* as a constant of truth, an aid in helping us successfully navigate through life.

*How does it do that?*

Let's say you're feeling afraid of stepping out of your comfort zone and applying for a job advancement. But (and this is a very big but) you feel your *North Star* nudging you to do it anyway.

What do you do?

## The Art Of Making A Good Decision

How do you know if it's the promptings of your *North Star* or just your own inner urges?

In the larger sense, how do you make a good decision?

Just as there's an art to many things in life, there's quite an art to good decision-making. It's something that can actually take a bit of practice to perfect but is well-worth mastering.

The art is in balancing the three elements of decision-making. These include:

1) **Your Rational Thought Processes.** This is the logical you, the "I graduated from school" you, the you who got through algebra, biology and all those horrendous final exams. And it's the same you who weighs the ups and downs of a situation, who thinks "if this, then that," and who figures the pluses and minuses of any given scenario.

2) **The Emotional You.** Not that you're necessarily an emotional person, but this refers to the way

you *feel* about something. Now, sure, feelings are hard to quantify. You can't put a ruler against a feeling. How your heart gets its input is probably tough to put into words anyway. But react to a situation it certainly does. And while sometimes those reactions can be as romantic as an old-time movie, the heart can be surprisingly astute and perceive a situation *exactly* as it is.

3) **Your** *North Star.* This could probably be filed under "inspiration." You could be standing around when you suddenly get this great answer to a problem you've been struggling with. It just pops into your head. Whatever you call it—your *North Star*, your moral compass, your conscience—it seems to be an *external* impetus that appears when you most need it. Then, afterwards, you feel *peaceful* about it. That's one of the telltale signs. There's a caveat though: You need to pay attention to these ideas when they appear and *act on them*. If you don't, future inspiration may no longer pay you a visit.

So now that you've identified these three elements, what comes next?

## The Sequence Of Decision-Making

There's a certain sequence you could apply to good decision-making.

First, you probably want to use your rational self to look the situation up one side and down the other. Focus your mind on it. Remember *defensive pessimism*? Apply that and, if you want, write the pros and cons down on paper.

Sometimes just doing this alone will virtually hand you your decision.

Next, get in touch with your feelings. See how you *feel*

*"In the long run, we shape our lives, and we shape ourselves. The process never ends until we die. And the choices we make are ultimately our responsibility."*

—Eleanor Roosevelt—

about the decision *after* passing it through your rational screen. Are there emotional factors that could offset the bright light of logic?

Do you still *feel* like something could be a success even when it doesn't look so good on paper? That's an important sign.

Next, and ideally, take a little time to see how your initial assessment settles out...and to give yourself some space to receive that precious inspiration. Not that you have to take weeks or months here. Just a little time.

During that period, be especially sensitive to any ideas that may pop into your head.

Finally, having already performed a lot of decision-making work, go someplace quiet, turn things over in your mind for a few minutes, *then make the decision right there and then.*

Some people make the decision, then take time to pray/ponder/meditate about it to see if they get a confirmation. A good, optimistic sense in response to this reflection is often interpreted as a "yes."

A dull, dark, even forgetful feeling is usually a "no."

---

**PRACTICAL TIP:** Does good decision-making still seem a bit intimidating? Here's a little exercise that may make you more aware of the dynamics going on here.

Go someplace quiet. Reflect on an upcoming decision. Think of the worst possible choice you could make relative to it...*then pretend you've just made that wrong decision.* Yes, the wrong decision.

How does *that* make you feel?

Is there an uproar going on inside you? Can you see exactly what a wrong decision feels like? Can you identify and file this "bad-choice response" away so you know how a wrong decision makes you feel...and, conversely, how a right decision would make you feel?

Next, reflect on the great decisions you've made in your life. Can you remember the pros and cons associated with those decisions? How does this new decision feel in relation to those gems?

Finally, ask yourself this: *What kind of decision would I make if I knew I couldn't fail?* If the answer is obvious, what's missing?

Courage?

Okay, class dismissed.

Good decision-making is the process of building trust with yourself. Like a plane's autopilot that keeps adjusting its course, zigzagging ever so slightly until it reaches its location, so too is your decision-making.

## Just Do It

As mentioned, when a thought or a decision brings you peace, fulfillment and courage, then you know it's likely you're heading toward your *Lighthouse*.

When your *North Star* prompts you to take a course of action, and you go through the above three steps to make a sound decision—but you're still feeling that fear—just follow through!

As our friends at Nike might say, *just do it!*

Remember, it's not courage without a little healthy fear present. That's just one of the keys of being at *The Helm*.

In the last couple of chapters, you've learned not to believe everything everyone else tells you. Or tries to foist upon you. Neither should you believe all the things that occupy your mind. A lot of it, maybe even most of it, has been mental illusion.

You also learned a bit about healthy, illusion-free decision-making.

Hopefully, I've given you some ways to live a truth-based (instead of illusion-based) existence.

In the next chapter, I'll share six warning flags that can help you identify the mental illusions you may be operating under.

*"We suffer primarily not from our vices or our weaknesses, but from our illusions. We are haunted, not by reality, but by those images we have put in their place."*

—Daniel J. Boorstin—

# Chapter 6

# ABOUT TO RUN AGROUND?

## *Six warning flags to heed.*

I've already mentioned how James Allen, author of the classic book, *"As a Man Thinketh,"* believes circumstances don't *make* the man, they *reveal* him.

Now here's how he compares your mind to a garden.

According to Allen, this "brain garden" of ours can either be well cared for or left to run wild, where the good stuff goes under-nourished and the weeds allowed to grow unabated. How different would your life be today if you had pulled those weeds of mental illusion years ago?

What if you had replaced them with seeds of truth, something that actually *supported* your dreams?

The question, as already touched on, is how do you tell the difference between a productive plant and a weed?

There are some self-awareness techniques that can help you out here. And that's what I want to touch on now with this...ahhh...revealing story.

# A Dip In The Ocean

It's our tenth anniversary. My wife and I head to Hawaii. I am beyond excited. We travel to the North Shore of Kauai, known for its big surf and beautiful steep beaches. We pull up to one, park, and I start racing for the shoreline.

As I run by an ample Hawaiian lady just sitting there, I yell "Aloha!" right in her face.

I'm ripping my shirt over my head now, kicking off my flip-flops, jumping into crystal, blue water and, yes, I am loving life.

After a while in the water, and amid my excitement, I notice out of the corner of my eye that the Hawaiians are now getting out of the ocean. "Something I said?" I yell, not really paying them much attention.

Even so, it does seem to be getting through to my brain that the surf is getting bigger and bigger.

And the undercurrent stronger and stronger.

This goes on until the glorious time I'm having playing in the Hawaiian surf gets smashed by wave after enormous wave. So, being the smart guy I am, I finally decide it's wiser to head back to the beach and wait the rough surf out.

So I start moving out of the water. But the Pacific has other ideas.

It's as if a carpet is getting pulled out from under my feet at 90 miles an hour. That's what the Hawaiian undertow can feel like. I promptly do a violent face-plant into the underwater sand before getting hurled back into the ocean.

Never, *never* in my life have I experienced anything like this. After re-gaining my feet, I try for the beach again but with the same scary results. I am sucked back in over and over!

*I cannot get out of this ocean!*

By now, my wife notices what's happening and enjoys what she believes is just me clowning around...and, all the while, I'm having this life-or-death wrestling match in the now hellish Hawaiian surf.

I am now officially panicking as the situation grows immeasurably worse. Swimming or walking isn't working, so I resort to crawling. But digging my claws into the sand doesn't help much.

This time, however, the surf takes it up a notch; *it eats my swimsuit!*

I do manage to snag the suit at my ankles but make a split-second decision to let it go to stay focused on my mortal struggle.

I'm now pretty certain I'm about to die. The naked, desperate me tries crawling out one more time but with the same desperate results. Back and forth and back and forth I go. My arms and legs flailing, my body being tossed bonelessly in the air, I look like a beach mime pantomiming a shark attack.

After seemingly endless repetitions of the same ocean torture, I finally figure out just the right formula of balance, traction and effort to drag myself out of there. Now exhausted and back on good, old terra firma, I let go of my last shred of pride and, while covering myself the best I can, limp for the safety of my towel.

To my front, there's my wonderfully sensitive, caring, nurturing spouse, now falling over herself in hysterical laughter—as is seemingly everyone else on the beach—while I furiously wrap the towel around me.

I yell, "Let's get out of here!" But that doesn't quiet her as we walk toward the car and pass the same ample Hawaiian woman sitting in the very same spot.

The woman raises her head, looks me in the eye and, with a beaming grin, screams...

"AAAALLLLOOOOOHHHAAAAA!!!"

## Lessons To Be Learned From This Shocking Tale Of Violence And Nudity

So now that I've completely humiliated myself again, what was the point of relating this sad, nearly tragic story?

Well, first off, I had acted wholly on the *illusion* that I knew everything there was to know about this particular stretch of Hawaiian beach. That illusion, needless to say, nearly cost me my life.

Second, our illusions, like that undertow from hell, can keep pulling us back to a dangerous place, over and over again, at the great risk of our time and health.

Third and, again, like me fighting that undertow, it takes focused, consistent and sometimes resourceful effort to break free of our illusions and return to a state of normalcy, much as it took everything I had just to return to land.

Fourth, and just as I was willing to surrender my bathing suit to the sea to focus on saving my life and then run like a not-so-little boy for the safety of my towel, you may have to want "normalcy" and truth so much you're willing to risk everything—yes, even temporary embarrassment—to achieve your end. So what are you willing to let go of (hopefully, not a swimsuit) to make room for something new and different? In my case, I traded my swimsuit for my life.

Likewise, in a very real sense, what you let go of can give you new life.

Before any of this can take place, though, you first need to be aware that you're actually stuck in a dangerous undertow. And that, amazingly enough, can take some self-examination.

*What thought keeps sucking you back into your own ocean of illusion?* Here's a hint: Look at what gives you the most emotional pain in your life. Most people with an unexamined life have no clue what negative thoughts are contributing to their recurring pain.

Remember Socrates' advice, "The unexamined life is not worth living"?

Hopefully, by the end of this chapter, you'll have a much better idea of what's sucking you back in again and again.

## Emotional Pain
## To Personal Gain

*"The truth is that our finest moments are most likely to occur when we are feeling deeply uncomfortable, unhappy, or unfulfilled. For it is only in such moments, propelled by our discomfort, that we are likely to step out of our ruts and start searching for different ways or truer answers."*

—M. Scott Peck—

As bad as it sometimes gets, *getting stuck in the undertow* can be absolutely necessary for your own personal growth.

Why? Because such a traumatic event creates *emotional pain*. And emotional pain is perhaps the greatest motivator known to mankind. It's the perfect fuel for learning.

No one likes to hear that, but it's true.

Consider the strategy of the successful insurance salesman's pitch. If the salesman tells you that life is good and an insurance policy will only make it better, chances are you'd just nod, say you'll think about it, and show the guy to the door.

If, however, he tells you how terrible things will be if your house burns down and you're uninsured, how you and your family could be homeless in an instant, and how everything you own could quickly go up in smoke, odds are better that you'd get out your pen and sign right there on the dotted line.

Pain trumps pleasure as a motivator. Always.

That said, let it light a little fire (no pun intended) under you to achieve greatness. Okay…back to those self-awareness techniques that may really help you out.

## Six Warning Flags
## Of Mental Illusion

So how do you become aware of *what you are not aware of?*

Here are six ideas to help. I call them the *"Six Running Aground Warning Flags."* They're designed to help you become aware of yourself enough to quickly change course.

And they work both on a personal and organizational level. You'll notice that each flag is *behavioral* in nature, so, as you read them, be aware of your emotional response to each.

The key is to tune into your emotions to receive the messages they're trying to give you.

# FLAG #1:
# You're A Finger-Pointer

If this is you, sad to say you make excuses, rationalize and blame others as well as yourself for your lack of happiness. See if any of this fits:

*It's your boss's fault that you're not enjoying your job; after all, she really is a jerk. It's your spouse's fault that you're bored in your relationship; he/she simply doesn't get you. It's the market's fault...your friend's fault... your pet Beagle's fault.*

Everyone's fault but your own.

Even so, blame can sometimes be subtle and hard for you, its author, to recognize. Yet it's often the cause for performance breakdowns and relationship break-ups. So try to stay open to ways you may unknowingly be playing the blame game.

## In Every Life A
## Little Rain Shall Fall

Look, life isn't fair and you know it.

Sometimes your boss really *can* be a jerk, your spouse really *can* be uncaring, and the market, your friends, even your pet Beagle really *can* cause you grief.

Unfair things happen to all of us all the time. They can take the form of any number of difficulties, including illness, accidents, uninformed decisions and their unintended consequences, nasty things others do to us, and a truckload of other major and minor infractions.

*"All blame is a waste of time. No matter how much fault you find with another, and regardless of how much you blame him, it will not change you. The only thing blame does is to keep the focus off you when you are looking for external reasons to explain your unhappiness or frustration. You may succeed in making another feel guilty about something by blaming him, but you won't succeed in changing whatever it is about you that is making you unhappy."*

—Wayne Dyer—

The question is, how will you respond to these bumps in the road?

Some of us choose to memorialize them, build shrines to them, and point to them whenever our present-day performance comes apart.

When you do that, though, you guarantee one thing: *Your progress in life will come to a complete standstill.*

## Don't Be A Victim

Excuses, rationalization and blame can lead to a sense of powerlessness. And that can lead to one of two destructive mentalities:

- **Victim Mentality:** This means living with a "powerless state of mind" where you don't believe you can control anything that happens in your life.

- **Victimizer Mentality:** Strangely enough, this is another powerless state of mind, but one that turns you into a bully. The underlying belief here is, "People are blocking me from success. I'm going to knock them out of my way."

In either case, you actually surrender your strength and subscribe to the belief that you are, in fact, powerless.

Think about it. When you blame, you assign your problems to someone or something else. *But how can you solve a problem that isn't your own?* You can't, and that's just the point.

A person blames because they don't want to be held responsible...but that *also disowns their ability to solve it.*

See how vicious the cycle is?

*"One reason so few of us achieve what we truly want is that we never direct our focus; we never concentrate our power. Most people dabble their way through life, never deciding to master anything in particular."*

—Anthony Robbins—

Who knows why unfairness is a part of virtually everyone's life? The great Author who designed this life appears to be a big fan of trials and difficulties, and how we respond to them.

But whatever the reason for unfairness, you need to take a deep breath, dismiss the impact your particular calamity has had on you...**AND GET ON WITH YOUR LIFE!**

Catch yourself whenever you feel the urge to blame. Stop the pity party. Redouble your efforts to take ownership of your challenges.

*You* are 100% responsible for how you think, feel and behave. No one else!

Remember, you can only point your finger when you take your hands off *The Helm*.

# FLAG #2:
# You Start Your
# Day Blindfolded

Here's where you have no focus, vision or goals for the day and just drift through the decades.

You're like a spore in the wind, going wherever the wind blows. You wake up really hoping the wind blows you someplace interesting that day because your life is so boring.

You may be at *The Helm* in all other respects...but you're piloting the ship with a blindfold on. It should come as no big surprise to you when you never reach desirable destinations.

Question: If you don't create your vision, who will?

You probably think the answer is no one, but you'd be wrong. In the vacuum of a missing self-imposed vision, *one will be provided for you by somebody else pretty much every single day!*

## Focus Theft

It could be the guy who cuts you off on the freeway, then gives you the middle finger salute. Or the jerk who sends you that nasty, profanity-filled email. Or the fact that you find your checking account inexplicably overdrawn $300.

If you haven't created a focus for the day, some incident, inconsequential as it may be, can quickly commandeer one for you.

So how do you create an unstoppable blowtorch of a focus?

At first, as with everything else, it may take some conscious effort. That's what habits are all about.

**PRACTICAL TIP:** Tonight identify your most important goals for tomorrow. You can even take a minute or two to jot them down, if you like.

That should help you wake up with purpose.

Then, tomorrow night, review your day's progress before thinking about your goals for the next day. See if you can identify how to improve on what you did. The whole thing doesn't have to take you five minutes.

Now this probably isn't exactly a new idea to you. But what may be new *is doing this every night for seven days*. What do they say about establishing a new habit? That you have to do something at least seven times in a row? Actually, true habits probably involve more like 21 days in a row, and longer, to really get established in your brain.

Even so, do this exercise for a week, and you'll lay the groundwork for a great habit. When you get the message that you expect yourself to be more focused and accountable every day—from the moment you open your eyes to the moment you close them—you'll be able to accomplish more and live a more directed life (might even help you sleep better at night).

You'll be better able to take life by *The Helm*.

*"A man who is master of himself can end a sorrow as easily as he can invent a pleasure. I don't want to be at the mercy of my emotions. I want to use them, to enjoy them, and to dominate them."*

—Oscar Wilde—

# FLAG #3:
## You Feel Emotionally Sick To Your Stomach

Here's where you have no claim to a sense of peace. You seem to be stuck in a lonely, empty and aching place.

As previously discussed, your emotions are your best gauge for knowing whether or not you're homing in on your *Lighthouse*.

Question: What dominant emotion do you feel right now?

Whether it's positive or negative, you're actually attracting more of the same right this very second.

Why? Because emotion attracts emotion. Negative attracts negative. Positive attracts positive. Again, it comes down to that famous Biblical scripture, "as you sow, so shall you reap."

Put another way, you *are* your dominant emotion.

### What's *Your* Operating System?

Here's another way to think of it.

What's *your* computer's operating system? You know... the super duper OS that drives your Mac or PC? Well, just like your computer, you have an operating system, too.

When it's negative, expect negative stuff to come out of it.

When it's positive, expect positive stuff to come out of it.

Like your computer, this is the way you operate, your orientation, the point of view everyone who comes in contact with you faces. Since negativity is almost always

*"We are masters of the unsaid words, but slaves of those we let slip out."*

—Winston Churchill—

associated with failure—and you happen to have a negative operating system—you might want to consider scrapping it and installing a much-needed upgrade.

That's true whether you're a PC or Mac person.

# FLAG #4:
# Mouthing Off

I just got through saying how negative attracts negative. Likewise, as a product of your thinking, your words also attract success or failure.

So, getting right down to it, *what comes out of your mouth?*

You know what I mean...do you often say negative or inappropriate things?

If so, you need to pay particularly close attention to that. Because it's the quickest way people get to know who you are and what you're after in life.

Take swearing, for example.

*Is there ever such a thing as positive swearing?*

Could you ever get away with saying something like, "Man, that Bob. He's one (fill in the blank with profanity) wonderful guy?"

Or, "Now *that* was a (fill in the blank with profanity) neat ballet performance."

See what I mean? Even if you try using profanity as an adjective to amplify something good, it always comes out negative.

But it doesn't have to be swearing. It can be a full range of negative things you could blurt out. When negative words emerge from your mouth, they imply a couple of things about you, whether right or wrong, right off the bat. These can include...

- You have such a limited grasp on the English language that you need profanity to cover that gaping hole in your descriptive vocabulary...not exactly the kind of impression you want to leave on upscale corporate colleagues.

- You grew up in such a rough environment that you're virtually stuck back there, at that ancient time and place, and can't make the adjustment to your present-day circumstances and the kind of culture that can now help you make gigantic leaps forward in life.

- You're so mired in the negativity habit that you no longer even realize what you're saying and who you're offending (undoubtedly someone who can play an important role in your life).

Negative words of any type can be a real buzzkill. What do I mean by that? When you enter a room, does the mood seem to nosedive? Do people get real quiet real quickly? Worse, do they get up and leave?

Are you seldom asked anything that would elicit a lengthy reply?

**PRACTICAL TIP:** Remember that counting exercise we did a few chapters ago? Well, dig it out again. Consciously count how many times you use a negative word, sentence or profanity in the next 24 hours (it's unlikely you'd utter negative words while sleeping, so don't worry about then).

If you stay with it, you'll soon see your "negative utterances" drop from, say, 20 to 15 to 10 to 5 to none a day. But you'll need to stay mildly dedicated.

I'm serious here.

Install a negative word detector in the OS of your brain, and you'll have potentially changed your entire destiny.

## Your Words
## Reflect Your Thoughts

Bottom line, the words you're using today *are* creating your future.

Literally. Consonant by consonant. Syllable by syllable.

I'm actually pretty good at predicting the future. All I have to do is listen to the words someone says, and I can predict their future with 95% accuracy.

*"To understand the world one must not
be worrying about one's self."*

—Albert Einstein—

# FLAG #5:
## Other People's Needs Aren't Anywhere On Your Radar Screen

Do you treat people like things?

Are you devoid of caring?

Something like that can just creep up on you. Often it's the result of bitterness leaking into your life... or a lack of self-esteem...or a mounting selfish and narcissistic nature.

Remember Scrooge? That humbug thing he had going on?

Old Scrooge's heart had grown as cold as a sack of snow. His response to the trials and sadness he suffered in his early years was to grow greedier and more selfish. One casualty of this unfortunate downturn in his nature was the love of his life.

From then on, Ebenezer, this man of business, really hardened his heart. A more caustic and uncaring soul never existed.

Can you relate? Does your world revolve entirely around you? Are you consumed by your own interests, details and business matters?

Is anyone or anything in your way looked upon as the enemy?

Do you see people as necessary annoyances that must be dealt with? Do you have little energy for them...but strangely enough, all the energy in the world to do the things that interest you?

On the home front, if you have kids, do you do everything you can to get them out of your hair so you can go back to "your own life?"

*"It is a wretched taste to be gratified with mediocrity when the excellent lies before us."*

—Isaac D'Israeli—

Do you find yourself building walls to separate yourself from those you should only be growing closer to? Does the sentence, "I know I've run aground when I can no longer empathize with others," hit home?

And how exactly is this "the-world-revolves-around-me" attitude of yours—if you actually suffer from it—working out at your job?

What's the definition of empathy anyway? *www.wikipedia.com* defines it as: "The capacity to recognize or understand another's state of mind or emotion. It is often characterized as the ability to put oneself in another's shoes..."

Well...*can* you put yourself in another's shoes?

Or are you just fine in those expensive cross-trainers of yours?

# *FLAG #6:*
# *Are You Buddy-Buddy With Mediocrity?*

Here's where you end up with ho-hum results yet, somehow, it's never quite your fault. That's so despite the fact that you were present at every "crime scene."

For you, success is fleeting. So is meaning and happiness—they all seem so capricious, so ready to flee from you like a cat from a wild toddler. You work hard but not smart. You only do what is expected of you, no more, no less. You never try to perfect anything—it just isn't in your job description. And you rarely take time to evaluate your results in order to get it better the next time. Who cares about that?

It's like that classic definition of insanity:

*Someone who keeps doing the same thing over and over but expects an entirely different result.*

**PRACTICAL TIP:** Not sure where you stand on the mediocrity scale? Take a second to evaluate your efforts (on a scale of 1-10 with 10 being the best) on the following:

a) home front (family/kids/spouse) _____
b) work arena _____
c) spiritual _____
d) personal growth _____
e) social areas in your life _____
f) physical _____

How did you do? Did you give yourself any 8s, 9s or 10s?

Or just a whole bunch of 4s, 5s and 6s?

If you're not getting the results you want, *don't keep doing the same things in the same ways.* Change.

Challenge yourself. Budget more time for tasks that are more challenging. Focus a little more. Shut the TV off every once in a while.

Take smart risks from time to time. Act on faith. That's what faith is for.

## Getting The Checkered Flag?

Okay, so which of these *Six Warning Flags* speaks to you?

It's okay to admit it to yourself. I generally find that, at any given time, one of these flags is speaking to me.

Well...maybe more like two or three.

Take the time to recognize the flags. Doing so can keep you from running aground.

In the next chapter, we'll learn how one small idea can have a huge impact on your life.

*"To dream anything that you want to dream. That's the beauty of the human mind. To do anything that you want to do. That is the strength of the human will. To trust yourself to test your limits, That is the courage to succeed."*

—Bernard Edmunds—

# Chapter 7

# BECOMING UNSTOPPABLE:

## *Go small to go BIG!*

You become unstoppable in the pursuit of your dreams the moment you surrender yourself to helping others achieve theirs—nothing can stop this human spirit of greatness.

It all starts with one small decision.

I was privileged to witness a character breakthrough in—of all places—*a garage sale*.

Do you like garage sales? They're where you actually get to pay someone to relieve them of their junk. Don't get me wrong, I think garage sales are great fun. My family and I love them. They're like treasure hunts.

Well, sort of.

One sunny Saturday we did the garage sale thing. We found a particularly large one, with hardly a square foot of lawn not covered by old rusty and dusty treasures. In fact, it looked like we had just come upon an antique store that exploded. I looked over the disorganization half-expecting a speaker to announce, "Clean-up on Lawn #9."

Whatever the sale's author chose to label it, he was definitely serious about conducting some sort of business that day.

"Wow, you've got more stuff than all the other garage sales put together," I told him.

"I know," he replied. "I've got to make some money today because I'm singing on *American Idol*. I need every penny I can scrape up to get to L.A."

"Good one. And I'm playing Stallone's boxing opponent in the next *Rocky*."

The guy chuckled. "No, I'm serious. I really am singing on *American Idol*."

"Whoops. Sorry about that. Thought you were kidding. Hey, let's hear a song."

I didn't expect much from this stout, little man but stood transfixed as he sang a gorgeous, passionate melody of songs, including the theme song of *Man of La Mancha*. It wasn't just his voice. It was something else; his energy, his gusto, his absolute lack of inhibition. No question, the guy was really good, a wonderful showman.

I stood super-glued to his lawn.

"Wow, you *do* have a great voice."

"Thanks," he said, then matter-of-factly handed me an old, dusty typewriter and said, "So why not buy this and…"

*Oh brother*, I thought, chuckling at the bait I just took.

But that didn't interrupt his sales pitch any, "…It doesn't work, but the parts are still good. Here, take it; you'll be glad you did. Just twenty bucks. And here's the stand…"

His "assumptive sale" approach now winding down, he kept throwing in morsels of his story. He always loved to sing and dreamt of singing on a well-lit stage to a huge audience. However, in the eighth grade, guys in the school choir made fun of his maturing, cracking voice—especially when he put some real oomph into it—saying he had a voice "only a deaf mother could love."

To avoid further humiliation, he vowed never to sing again. And he remained true to that vow, at least the part about not singing in public. Remember about the labels others stick on us? Well, it was that decision, *that one little decision*, that left a gigantic impact on his love for singing.

In one little decision he had given up his greatest passion.

Then one night after watching *American Idol*, he realized how much he missed singing. He decided to sing loud and majestically in the shower. After he got out and toweled himself down, he told his wife that he wanted to sing on the show.

She laughed, "Yeah, wouldn't that be neat?"

"No, I'm serious."

"What are you talking about? You don't even sing."

Why did she say that? Because he couldn't sing? No, because she'd never heard him sing in all the years they'd been together. Not in the shower, not in the car, not at birthday parties, not anywhere.

He told me that, while watching a particularly good singer on *American Idol*, he felt like he was sitting in the audience watching someone else perform *his* songs.

"No more!" he said, "That's it. Whether I make it or not, I'm going for it."

## Your Life Is Made Up Of Many Small Decisions—Many Small, *Critically Important* Decisions

You may say that it was no small decision for my friend to sing on *American Idol*. But let's back it up a bit. Remember when it all started for him?

*When he sang in the shower.*

It was this small decision, this tiny, little choice, that led him to try out for the show.

I believed then, as I do now, that *when a person lets go of their fears and decides to take The Helm, not only are they propelled to greatness, they can become unstoppable. When you have the courage to listen to your heart—and it may be a very small voice—you become an irresistible force of nature.*

He handed me a decrepit-looking eight-track tape player accompanied by three equally dubious tapes. "You'll need this as well. I think it's a collectors' item or something."

I walked away from that garage sale with a broken typewriter—with really good parts, mind you—an eight-track player with three worn tapes that may or may not be from the Cowsills, an ancient TV with a funky knob, and a few other items my wife actually wanted.

What I left behind was the $100 bill I had packed in my wallet in the event I actually came across something worthwhile at a garage sale. "I have no change," he held up his hands in protest.

"That's okay. It's yours. May the force be with you," I muttered and shook his hand.

He had taken *The Helm* of his good ship, listened to his *North Star*, and steered toward his *Lighthouse* on a voyage of good fortune. I was honored to help finance his dream.

I took his junk home and threw it all away for him (isn't that our understanding with the garage sale people?).

Although I never saw him again, either around his neighborhood or on *American Idol*, I'm convinced he made a better life for himself.

## The Stage Is Set, The Curtain Is Rising—*Where The Heck Are You?*

Small decisions open or close off our lives.

At some seemingly unimportant moment in your history, did you unknowingly make a permanent decision to give up something dear to you?

One small decision? One altered life?

*Whether you realize it or not, you're probably making small, almost imperceptible decisions right this very moment. Sure, there's the everyday stuff. Are you going to the store? Can you squeeze a workout in? Are you taking your son to karate? Your daughter to dance? Do you want salad with your salmon? Or fries with your Big Mac?*

But mixed among those mundane choices may be one of much larger significance.

*Are you going to look into school? Check out that new job? Start burning off more calories than you take in? Get that presentation together? Begin writing that novel you've always wanted to write?*

A little decision like that can easily get shuffled to the back burners...or, on the other hand, acted on right there and then. Just like my garage sale singing buddy who listened to the quiet voice of his *North Star* in the shower and made the small yet enormous decision to start singing again.

Performing for *American Idol* must have, at least at some point in his life, seemed impossible to him. But I presume he did it anyway. *So how do you do the seemingly impossible?*

It starts with this kind of tiny desire and decision.

## Are You Just "Slightly" Off Course?

Dieter F. Uchtdorf, formerly a chief pilot and senior vice president of flight operations for *Lufthansa*, told this story in a recent talk:

"In 1979, a large passenger jet with 257 people on board left New Zealand for a sightseeing flight to Antarctica and back. Unknown to the pilots, however, someone had modified the flight coordinates a mere two degrees. This error placed the aircraft 28 miles (45 km) to the east of where the pilots assumed they were. As they approached Antarctica, the pilots descended to a lower altitude to give the passengers a better look at the landscape. Although both were experienced pilots, neither had made this particular flight before and had no way of knowing that the incorrect coordinates placed them directly in the path of Mount Erebus, an active volcano that rises from the frozen landscape to a height of more than 12,000 feet (3,700 m)."

"As the pilots flew onward, the white of the snow and ice covering the volcano blended with the white of the clouds above, making it appear as though they were flying over flat ground. By the time the instruments sounded the warning that the ground was rising before them, it was too late. The airplane crashed into the side of the volcano, killing everyone on board."

"It was a terrible tragedy brought on by a minor error—a matter of only a few degrees."

Sad story, but a powerful example of the differences small changes in life can make.

A little, *continual* change can mean you reach your destination...or miss it catastrophically.

Little changes over time will tell your story.

## Where Baby Steps Can Lead You

If you're like millions of others, you've probably tried losing weight at some point in your life. For many, it's a daunting, frustrating task.

So here's the question: Who do you think would be more successful at this?

Someone who's sick of feeling fat and decides right on the spot to launch a fitness blitzkrieg of exercising at 5:00 in the morning, six times a week, eating better and getting eight hours of sleep at night?

Or...the person who starts small and decides to walk maybe twice a week for 15 minutes before even thinking about going harder?

*The odds greatly favor the person who understands the "Go Small To Go Big" principle.*

*Go Small To Go Big*, in connection with exercise, simply means starting small to bypass your brain's alarm system. You know...the alarm that says you can't do this because you've always failed at it before?

Starting small instead of the usual "going-all-out-all-at-once" method helps you sneak up on yourself. It gives you the early momentum and quick, initial success you may have missed all those other times.

You see, change, even for the better, sets off your internal *fight-or-flight* alarm. That's something built into you to help you deal with perceived threats. In this instance, setting too large an exercise goal—like trying to follow that famous triathlon athlete's workout, for example, when you have trouble just walking to the mailbox—is perceived as a threat.

A rather large one.

And it's a guaranteed way to sabotage yourself.

## Hot And Cold Analogies

Sure, many will tell you that it's ridiculous to think you can get physically fit by walking a couple times a week. And maybe they'd be right if that were all there were to it. However, and as mentioned, it's not just muscles or endurance you're trying to build at this stage.

It's momentum.

Think snowball effect. A little snowball rolling down the hill and building momentum every foot of the way soon becomes a big snowball, then a bigger snowball, then, in no time, a huge threat to anyone in its path.

Want a warmer analogy? Okay, how about starting a campfire? You put a bunch of twigs, maybe some dry bark or leaves in a pile, then light it. It catches fire, so you start putting bigger stuff on it. In no time at all, you have a bunch of logs blazing away.

What would have happened if you tried starting the fire using a log first?

Nothing, that's what.

But that's just the way of momentum. It starts small and builds on itself.

I remember, as a young guy, getting stuck in a snow-filled church parking lot. I kept gunning the engine, spinning the wheels and, effectively, digging myself in deeper. That's when a church member who happened to be an engineer knocked on my window. "Go as slowly as you can. Just barely move the tires. Be easier for you to gain traction that way."

Sure enough, I touched the gas just enough to get the wheels turning and, lo and behold, the tire rubber was able to engage the snow at that slower speed and move the vehicle. Once I got moving, it was easier to build momentum from there. I never forgot that lesson.

You don't need big decisions, big efforts, to get big results. At least at the start. Remember Einstein's 15-minute-a-day learning habit? *Anyone can be a genius if they pick one specific subject and study it diligently just 15 minutes each day for a year?*

That's starting small.

How long do you think it took the Colorado River to cut the Grand Canyon?

It's all about momentum.

## Find Your Entry Point

The seemingly impossible becomes possible when you start small.

> *Through the cumulative effect of life's small decisions, your human spirit of greatness opens the doors to miracles...and that's when you become unstoppable.*

What *small* decision do you need to make today to get started?

*"Man does not simply exist, but always decides what his existence will be, what he will become in the next moment."*

—Viktor Frankl—

You say this small decision still causes you stress? Fine. Go smaller. Even to the point of being ridiculous. Remember how slowly I had to move my car tires?

What you're looking for here is an entry point.

Recall that whole thing about a journey of a thousand miles beginning with a first step? Well...*find your first step*. It doesn't have to bear any resemblance to the kinds of steps you'll be taking later on.

It's just your very first step in the direction you want to go.

## The Impossible Dream, One Step At A Time

All those baby steps of yours can add up to something incredibly impressive. Maybe even "impossible."

One of my definitions of the impossible is *doing something you really don't think can be done...yet your North Star nudges you to do it anyway.*

Remember the famous song, *The Impossible Dream*? Why didn't Joe Darion write *these* lyrics?

> *To dream the possible dream*
> *To fight the beatable foe*
> *To bear with minor league sorrow*
> *To run where it's never dangerous to go*

> *To right the misdemeanor wrong*
> *To be found pure and chaste from afar?*
> *To try when your arms aren't especially weary*
> *To reach something well within your grasp*

Doesn't have quite the same ring to it, does it? My new lyrics are, safe to say, pretty mediocre. Uninspiring. Certainly nothing to rouse your spirit and make you fasten your seatbelts, correct?

*"You will become as small as your controlling desire, or as great as your dominant aspiration."*

—James Allen—

Men and women will often rise to a challenge. On the other hand, if the challenge isn't much of anything, people will often just shrug and go their own way.

Just for clarity's sake, let's look at the original lyrics from *The Impossible Dream*.

*To dream the impossible dream*
*To fight the unbeatable foe*
*To bear with unbearable sorrow*
*To run where the brave dare not go*

*To right the unrightable wrong*
*To love pure and chaste from afar*
*To try when your arms are too weary*
*To reach the unreachable star*

*This is my quest*
*To follow that star*
*No matter how hopeless*
*No matter how far*

*To fight for the right*
*Without question or pause*
*To be willing to march into hell*
*For a heavenly cause*

Wow. "To be willing to march into hell for a heavenly cause." When was the last time you felt *that* way?

Or have you ever felt that way?

This music is inspiring...enlightening...motivating... adventurous...even fun.

Consider this quote attributed to Ferdinand Magellan.

"The sea is dangerous and its storms terrible, but these obstacles have never been sufficient reason to remain ashore...Unlike the mediocre, intrepid spirits seek victory over those things that seem impossible...It is with an iron will that they embark on the most daring

> *"To change one's life: start immediately. Do it flamboyantly. NO exceptions!"*
>
> —William James—

of all endeavors...to meet the shadowy future without fear and conquer the unknown."

You remember Magellan from your elementary school history, right? The first maritime explorer to ever circumnavigate the globe? Yeah, that guy.

I doubt anyone would ever accuse him of being mediocre.

The stage lights are on, the curtain is raised and the audience is waiting in anticipation.

*Where the heck are you?*

---

**PRACTICAL TIP:** Here's an exercise that might help you see where to take your first baby step.

Okay—and remember this is just an exercise now—pretend you've just been given a death sentence. You've contracted a fatal disease and have maybe a month or two left to live.

Looking back over your life from this rare perspective, *what would you have done differently?*

Would you have taken more chances? Not been so afraid to try new things?

Maybe you would have eaten more lobster, learned to play the harp, been an expert on the Civil War, rode more roller coasters, laughed more, cried more, been less afraid—only you know. The point here is, in looking at your life in retrospect and from this "final" perspective, it may be easier for you to identify the things you really do love and that make you the happiest…as well as those things you'd want to avoid at all costs.

Okay, presto-chango! The good news is you're not going to die after all (at least I hope you're not). And, now, after earnestly reflecting on this topic for a quiet half-hour (now that you're getting better at doing that half-hour reflective thing), and with a firm grasp on what will make you happier, *the stage is set for you to incorporate these ideas into the way you live your life from this moment on.*

## One Small Decision Away

What seemingly small decision can you make right now to start living your own *Impossible Dream*?

In this chapter, we've discussed how your life is determined not so much by huge decisions, but by the cumulative effect of small, almost under-the-radar ones.

You are literally one small decision from getting front and center on the stage of life. One small decision away from pursuing your goals, dreams and hopes.

*One small decision!*

What has your *North Star* been nudging you to do? What have you been putting off? Maybe it's…

…an urge to look into a new interest, a new skill, a new career

…re-committing yourself to a positive attitude at work regardless of what others think-

...accepting that your team needs a leader more than a friend

...holding others accountable, but in a kind sort of way

...building better relationships with your spouse, kids or loved ones

...asking for forgiveness and ridding yourself of pride; learning to be less "me" oriented

...learning to let go, surrender and trust God with things you can't control

...taking better care of yourself

Think there's more to your life than what's been on the screen so far? Think you've stagnated and are now just going through the motions?

The next chapter talks about a serious life challenge I had...and how my response to it may be your way out, too.

---

*"Every day you may make progress. Every step may be fruitful. Yet there will stretch out before you an ever-lengthening, ever-ascending, ever-improving path. You know you will never get to the end of the journey. But this, far from discouraging, only adds to the joy and glory of the climb."*

—Winston Churchill—

*"We must never forget that we may also find meaning in life even when confronted with a hopeless situation, when facing a fate that cannot be changed. When we are no longer able to change a situation...we are challenged to change ourselves."*

—Viktor Frankl—

# Chapter 8

# HAVE YOU SOLD YOUR SOUL?

Possibly the most liberated force in all of nature is a child.

Think about it. What holds a child back? Oh sure, mom and dad. But that's only on the surface. The stuff that goes on behind the scenes and between the ears of a child is absolutely uninhibited.

Children are free spirits without any of the "maturity" controls installed. As such, kids live in the moment, not handicapped by any such constraints.

I recall the year Santa brought me that red bike I so wanted. I loved that BMX bike so much, I even kept it near my bed when I went to sleep at night! I remember riding it around, popping wheelies, doing bunny hops, and going off jumps. I even organized a neighborhood bike patrol where we'd cruise the neighborhood looking for would-be robbers, talking on our walkie-talkies, looking so very official and important. I even made a real police siren sound that drove the neighbors crazy.

Poor old Marina Duffin called my mom asking her to make me stop doing it because it was raising her blood pressure.

But not raising an adult's blood pressure isn't exactly high on a kid's priority list. What does rank high is unbound creativity and a staggering zest for life.

Both flow freely.

We're all born with this beautiful childhood passion and an amazing ability to savor the present. Our thoughts were not attached to any outcomes, remember that? Yet somehow, over the process of getting older, this passion got replaced with fear, complacency and exhaustion.

Sadly, over time, the wonderful childlike part of us dies, and we are reborn as over-anxious adults.

## You're So Childish

Not everyone's childhood dies, though.

Some wise individuals still find ways to nurture that glorious part of themselves—the enthusiasm, free-thought, energy and God-given ability to "try." So the question here is, what percentage of childhood freedom and passion do you still have left in your tank?

On a scale of 1-10 (with 10 being the highest), rank how much **childlike freedom and passion** is still left in you. Go ahead.

(We're pausing here while you do that.)

Okay...what's your score? If you ranked at, say, 5 or under, do you think it's still possible to boost it up to an 8 or 9?

What follows is an experience I had with someone who taught me that such a thing is still entirely possible.

## Steel-Coated Marshmallows

Can your life change in a blink of an eye? How about half a blink? For either the good or the bad?

I think it can. Have you heard the number 119104? It probably means nothing to you...just what comes after 119103 and before 119105.

But this number would literally revolutionize my life in one miraculous moment and reconnect me to an internal freedom I thought I'd lost forever.

On the outside I appeared to have it all. I'd been recruited to be the chief operating officer/executive director for a company that offered services nationwide to large Fortune 500 companies. In short order, we were able to quadruple the size of the company and continue to grow it at a phenomenal rate.

I was happily married with two beautiful children, active in my church, and even had a little Beagle puppy...yet, truth was, I was miserable.

I felt stressed, as though, internally, I was running 100 miles an hour on a treadmill to nowhere. Sure, I'd been doing all the right corporate things, touched all the right bases. But below the surface it seemed meaningless and exhausting.

I had become a steel-coated marshmallow.

Deep down inside, I didn't really believe I deserved the success I was having. Interestingly enough, I was later to learn that these kinds of sentiments are not uncommon among high-level, highly paid executives.

I was losing myself, becoming someone I wasn't very proud of (which is not to say I was doing anything immoral or wrong, just violating the call of my *North Star*).

I had, in effect, let go of *The Helm*.

Despite being blessed with great success as the COO of this company, I was in way over my head and I knew it. My heart had slowly grown hard and void of the gratitude I should have had with my abundance.

My soul had shrunk in the presence of corporate America, in other words.

Stress was coming at me from three fronts, with the CEO and senior VP of the company demanding more customers and sales even as frustrated employees nipped at me from below. It was like getting pecked to death by a flock of crazed pigeons.

One reason for the stress was that my employees were making life-and-death decisions every single day. Literally. If they screwed up, not only could there be an unthinkable loss in human terms, it could mean a huge litigation for the company...and my head getting handed to me on a platter.

No offense at all to genuine POWs, but it was like I was another kind of POW—a *Prisoner of Work*.

I actually reached the point where I considered selling out, compromising much of what I believed. As if that wasn't enough, more was coming down the pike.

## Build It And The Stress Will Come

At this bizarre point in my life, my wife and I decided to build a house.

Not sure why. Really, I'm no masochist. But if you ever find yourself bored, go build a house ☺. I promise you your life will instantly be packed with a sea of bewildering details, inexplicable costs, non-stop phone calls and moments of sheer terror.

We had been saving our money for years and, after extensive research, found the perfect place to build, the perfect contractor, and were excited to finally begin building our perfect home.

Things went incredibly well. For the first 36 hours.

That's when, bless our "perfect" little contractor's heart, he decided to forge our names on a check and steal tens of thousands of dollars from us.

It seemed like just a day later when liens were filed, foreclosure notices posted, and a five-year lawsuit was kicked off.

Not exactly what we had in mind when we planned our dream house.

Rightfully so, I felt out of control, angry and downright powerless.

## Wake Up Calls:
## Not A Matter Of If, But When

I was struggling to breathe at work and gasping for breath at home.

The most difficult part was watching my wonderful wife lie awake at night wondering how we were going to survive this financial tsunami. She had been so cute in her excitement to build our dream, visualizing the paint color in every room, the decorations and the furniture... now it had all vanished in embezzlement.

But we hadn't hit bottom just yet.

One day during this time, my son fell and hit his head, and my wife took him to the hospital. Shortly afterward, while in a meeting, I got this emergency phone call from my wife. She told me about my son then said, "They've done a CT scan and an MRI and believe they've found a large brain tumor."

Life stopped dead in its tracks. In half a blink of my eye.

Ever get a call like that? Were you at work or in public at the time? If not, I can tell you, it borders on the surreal. Something strange happens to your senses; it's like everything takes on this cruel glare and time slows by half.

I laid the phone down, excused myself, and told my legs to move me out of the building and toward my car.

Life has this charming way of slapping you upside the head when you're not at *The Helm*.

*Mariners will tell you that you're either in the middle of a storm, just coming out of one, or getting ready to go into one—that's the way of the sea. And life.*

## Meanwhile, Back At The Parking Lot...

I got in my car and started it up, but confess now to have driven entirely on autopilot. I was struggling, of course, with the horrifying concept that my son, my little buddy, might have a life-threatening brain tumor.

At the hospital (fortunately, my good, old autopilot had delivered me safely there), we finished all the paperwork, set up appointments for further testing, and left to head for home. The drive was extremely quiet.

Everyone else went to bed after that exhausting day. I was physically and emotionally spent, but too restless to lie down. Thoughts curled around my heart like tentacles. I needed to do something, but what? TV, as is often the case, was of zero solace to me, and I was way too amped up to sit and think.

Then I happened to notice our family photo album. I began thumbing through it.

The photos were hard-wired to my heart, something tough to put into words. There was my little buddy, his big brown eyes, golden blond hair and unlimited potential clearly evident on his beautiful, innocent features.

I was drowning in a pool of emotion.

My first thought was that this could be the beginning of the end for my family. Life, after all, isn't a dress rehearsal. There are no guarantees. We might not have a second chance at survival.

At that moment, I had reached a place of total honesty. All the extraneous stuff, the illusions, the vanity, the pride and the pettiness were stripped away.

What was left was my naked soul.

Ironically, this rare state of humility is fertile soil to plant new seeds. I was now ready to wake up and take my life back. If ever there were an opportunity to take back *The Helm*, this was it.

But...*exactly how?*

Have you ever had one of these life-changing moments? A difficult time when, strangely enough, you could clearly see through all the illusions and deceptions? It's like the lyrics of that Steve Winwood song, "While You See a Chance":

*When there's no one left to leave you*
*Even you don't quite believe you*
*That's when nothing can deceive you*

But now I had to do something about it.

## The Hero Is Missing In Action

When my wife and I started having kids, I made one goal that would end up defining my life: I decided to be remembered for being *a great daddy, a hero in the lives of my children and wife.*

The reality was, though, I was far from it. I had lost my way. Somehow, I had taken the wrong roads enough times that I no longer knew where I was. I had broken the promise I'd made to God, my wife, the kids and myself. The pain at that moment was horrific. It felt like I was soaking the gaping wound of my soul in salt.

Worst-case scenarios played in a continuous loop in my brain. I never felt so afraid in my life. Nor felt more powerless.

The only power I did feel I had left was to pray and look to the heavens for help for my boy.

I mentioned taking back *The Helm*? Life was giving me a second chance to do just that. The challenges we face are there for a reason and, in fact, are tailor-made for our growth and learning. I realized that now and knew I still had the potential to lead with courage and unleash the love and warmth stuck deep inside me.

*I knew I still could be a hero to my family.*

## Not Becoming The Worst Of Your Parents

I had always promised myself I'd never be the father I had growing up...yet here I was behaving pretty much the same way.

As if it wasn't me, I heard myself saying the very same things my dad did: i.e. "Because I said so," "Kids are to be seen and not heard," etc. My father, sad to say, was an alcoholic during my younger years, making for a rather chaotic childhood (he no longer drinks, by the way, and has changed his ways).

Back then, he was distant, impatient, and nothing I ever did was good enough for him. I wanted so badly to make him proud of me, but that never happened.

Now I had become my father. Instead of the drinking, though, I used a corporate stress equivalent.

Have you ever caught yourself in the same "I'll never do that or say this" syndrome (only to later catch yourself, mid-sentence, saying the very same things you promised on a stack of Bibles you'd never say)?

I've since come to believe that this is a developmental stage of adulthood.

As I continued looking at the photo album that night, one question became emblazoned in my mind:

"Are you proud of yourself?"

The answer was clear.

How about you? Are you proud of the relationship you've had with the people who matter the most? Proud of the way you are at work? Proud of the thoughts that course through your brain? Proud of the way you spend your time?

*Are you a hero in the lives of the people you love most?*

## It's All A Numbers Game

I resolved that night to do what I needed to do to get back on track again. I wasn't sure how, like my garage sale friend. I just knew I would.

Now maybe this sounds like overly-done Hollywood stuff, but as I was putting the photo album away, I knocked a book off the shelf that I'd read back in graduate school.

It was *Man's Search for Meaning*.

I picked it up and thumbed through it, the highlights I had made in graduate school still standing out.

*And that's when I saw the number 119104.*

It was the number tattooed on the forearm of a hero of mine by the name of Viktor Frankl. He was a Jewish concentration camp survivor from WWII.

Miraculously, he had taken the number 119104, normally a symbol of unspeakable evil and atrocity, and transformed it into a personal symbol of power, courage and love inside that hellish prison.

He had accomplished something that, by all accounts, was entirely impossible:

*Frankl had established humanity in an inhuman setting.*

The instant Frankl's book fell off its shelf, my life changed. Something deep within me came back to life, awakened by his words. I figured that if Frankl could liberate himself in a death camp, surely I could liberate myself from my harsh but more *reasonable* challenges.

Life was giving me a wakeup call.

I was now at a crossroads; I had the opportunity to choose a brand-new path that could give new direction and fulfillment to my life—regardless of what would happen to my little boy. I realized then that I had no power over life and death, but held *all* the power I could ever want to choose how I would react to my circumstances.

## Another Kind Of POW

I'm happy to report that my son is alive and well today and driving us (contentedly) crazy.

Having made it through that crisis with a wonderfully happy ending, some important lessons were indelibly imprinted in my skull. One has to do with being, as I mentioned, a corporate prisoner of work.

Again, with absolutely no disrespect to real POWs—needless to say, these are heroic human beings worthy of our admiration—I'd like to apply this *Prisoner of Work* term to the working world.

So...do you think your boss wants you to be a POW? You might laughingly say, "Of course." But I think you'd be wrong.

Bosses really don't want overextended workers or Prisoners of Work. *Research shows that productivity actually goes down when employees are overextended.* What's more, exhausted, bedraggled people are not pleasant to be around, nor do they make good team players.

Fact is, the *Gallup Management Journal* estimated that only **29%** of workers are truly "engaged." Engaged, by their definition, is "working with passion and having a profound emotional connection to their company."

The troubling thing is, if that's anywhere close to being accurate, 71% of workers are not into their jobs at all. They are true POWs. That means these folks are wandering around in a zombie-like state of mind, going through those jerky, zombie movements while sabotaging the earnest efforts of the more dedicated people around them.

## Corporate POWs' Effect On Performance

Why do corporate POWs drag themselves around the office?

Simple. Living with the perception that you aren't in control of your life invites stress...and that can stimulate the old amygdala (the part of your brain responsible for the fight-or-flight response).

When your amygdala is always on hyper-alert, that's the definition of *chronic stress*. And when you're a victim of chronic stress, you're stuck in a numbing cycle of stress, anxiety and exhaustion.

Being a corporate POW invites the same kind of horrendous crisis I had.

If you're lucky.

If you aren't, your whole life can pass you by with you bent under this tremendous weight, month after month, year after year, and you not even realizing it. When you finally do retire under these miserable circumstances, if you even live that long, that's when it might finally smack you that you've actually missed out on your entire life.

Corporate POWs invite one of life's great, irreversible pains:

*Regret.*

Relationships fail, couples divorce, families break up, health goes out the window, finances run dry, lives crash and burn...but at least you've managed to be a corporate hero all your life, right?

Returning to my story, I had sold my soul as the COO. No question about that. What did it feel like? A profound sense of loneliness and discontent always keeps you

company. Distraction is the name of the game. I was always finding inventive ways to divert myself from the authentic issues at hand. Outdoor recreation, karate, video games, you name it, I did it, in the little amount of time I had off. Anything to avoid coming face-to-face with the promptings of my *North Star.*

When you turn your back on what makes you happiest, the only way you can feel good about yourself is to stay busy and distracted.

I was really good at that.

*"Your life is the sum result of all the choices you make, both consciously and unconsciously. If you can control the process of choosing, you can take control of all aspects of your life. You can find the freedom that comes from being in charge of yourself."*

—Attributed to Robert F. Bennett—

# Chapter 9

# OBSTACLE ILLUSIONS AND OTHER SELF-IMPOSED LIMITATIONS

"Give me liberty or give me death!"

Those famous words, delivered by Patrick Henry during the Revolutionary War, became the rallying cry that stirred the hearts of noble men and women back then. As important as that phrase was, it holds particular relevance today.

I'm referring here, of course, to your own *personal freedom*.

If you can't find that freedom, your spirit will eventually wither.

Personal freedom starts as a control issue. So who's in control of *your* life? Your corporate puppet-masters? Your obsessions? Your addictions? Your selfishness?

Or the healthy, balanced you?

It's only through *personal liberation* that you can wake up and take *The Helm*.

**PRACTICAL TIP:** Priorities. What are yours at this point? Take a deep breath, get out your pen, BE PAINFULLY HONEST, and rate the following aspects of your life (on a scale of 1-10, with 10 being your highest priority; you can use the same rating repeatedly). Don't put down what you think you should say, put down what you HONESTLY feel at this moment. Don't worry. We won't tell anyone.

- Nice, new Lexus _____
- Considered a miracle-worker at work _____
- A promotion and hefty raise _____
- Time with your kids or friends _____
- Prestige from your job _____
- Good relationships at work _____
- Good relations with your spouse/significant other _____
- Time to exercise _____
- Corporate perks _____
- Vacations _____
- Winning that bonus _____
- Reaching the next level at work _____
- Stock options _____

Okay, I obviously weighted this more with corporate goodies than family and relationship ones, but that was just to give you a broad check-up. So, tell the truth, did you rate business way above family?

Or did family trump business?

If you honestly did rate business above family, is this the way you want it? Did you *consciously* make that choice? Or did it kind of creep up on you?

And if you rated family above business, does your day-to-day life really reflect that? Or are you living a lie where you really aren't investing yourself in something you say is your priority?

Where you spend your time and energy tells the whole story.

## Meet A Noble Author

When I was alone in the family room during the night of my particular crisis, I continued reading *Man's Search for Meaning*. It was as though Viktor Frankl had written it just for me, just for that moment. I couldn't put it down.

**PRACTICAL TIP:** I recommend you read it, too. Even if you're not much of a reader, *Man's Search for Meaning* will touch you. Make yourself read the first hundred pages. I promise it will stir the spirit of greatness within you.

I was so moved by the man's noble display of the human spirit, I made up my mind to meet Viktor Frankl.

The thing was, I had no idea how popular he was. Frankl was a celebrity in his own right, a highly acclaimed international speaker, psychiatrist and best-selling author of millions and millions of books.

To make a long story short, my dream came true one snowy January day.

We talked about the book and his experiences in the death camps. Here was a man who, while a prisoner, lost everything near and dear to him. He was in a living hell; and yet, somehow, in this hell, he took the number 119104 and transformed it into a symbol of power, love and courage. That intrigued me. And I don't "intrigue" easily.

*Frankl really reached me!*

In his book, he talked about his experiences of survival against all odds. Despite those odds, the number 119104 would escape the death camp alive and intact. I was, needless to say, deeply moved by his perseverance in the face of the inhumane treatment he and others received. His stories overwhelmed me just as much then as they do now.

Yet, strangely enough, every time I read a page, *my soul was infused with energy and hope.*

## Keeping Your Hopes Alive

In our conversation, Frankl and I discussed how a person can gain control of his or her life in the midst of extreme circumstances.

Here you and I struggle to control our lives in relatively normal and abundant times, while Frankl managed to establish humanity under the most barbaric conditions.

How is that even done? How do you find meaning in a place specifically designed to kill you? Frankl found it by reaching out to others and *choosing* his attitude in any given moment. He strove *to create a bright spot in his day* by blessing the lives of others. As strange as it may sound, in this death setting, humor played a tremendous role in his survival.

Hope was also a common thread for those wanting to stay alive in the death camps. People who lost it soon shed the will to live and all too quickly died.

*Do you know someone who's lost hope?* While they're not likely to die from hopelessness, at least not as quickly as those in the camps did, they can soon become dead to living. The zombies, remember?

So the question is, how do you keep hope alive while being bombarded with major challenges? Or even not-so-major challenges (a constant barrage of minor annoyances can drive you crazy, too)?

*Frankl had seen tons of suffering, but it was never enough to kill the hope within him.*

Prisoners were regularly beaten and tortured, disease was rampant, it was bitterly cold, frostbite and starvation were constant companions, yet Frankl managed to maintain his hope and take *The Helm* to better serve others.

From somewhere within him, he intuitively knew that blaming the Nazis—or his fellow prisoners, for that matter—wasn't going to get him anywhere. So Frankl decided to take ownership of his life. He decided that if he couldn't resolve the problem of being a prisoner in a death camp (which certainly wasn't of his making), *he could at least own its impact on him.*

The death camp was certainly no illusion. It was all too real. All too brutal. But to give up hope and the desire to live because you were stuck in there was, in fact, an illusion.

I sometimes refer to these sorts of things as *"obstacle illusions."*

*"What is to give light must endure burning."*

—Viktor Frankl—

## Obstacle Illusions

Sure, this may be a nice play on words and all that...but it makes an important point.

Using Frankl's case as an example, an *obstacle* is a physical reality that cannot be denied...but an *illusion* may be an accompanying *belief* that appears to be real, but, in effect, *doesn't have to be.*

So an obstacle illusion is a self-limiting thought, a lie, anything that diverts you from your reality, your *Lighthouse.* For example, *if* Frankl believed that because he was weak, sick and starving (which was, in fact, the case) he no longer had any business having hope (an obstacle illusion), and he would have never been able to help ease the suffering of countless prisoners.

He would have just been numbered among the herd of walking dead.

Applying this to you, for example, you may have a boss who, you believe, never recognizes or respects you. He/she, then, is your obstacle (a physical reality) and the accompanying illusion is, "I hate my job and can never be happy or succeed here."

But does your illusion come close to the actual truth? It does, if you choose to believe it does. We talked about magicians earlier. They, of course, perform illusions in the name of entertainment. Their illusions *appear to be real, but are not.* Your eyes take in something that isn't completely the truth...in the same way an obstacle illusion is a thought that appears to be real, but, in fact, is not.

However if your *North Star* helps you spot these obstacle illusions, a whole new world can open up to you.

Take work, for example.

## Growing Through Workplace Challenges

It's probably fair to say that a good 95% of all business organizations have drama.

Most organizations have normal problems between normal people, departments and teams. The folks in any given business are human, after all, and can temporarily lose their way. Mostly, these are good people who lose their grip on *The Helm*—something that can be corrected or, at the very least, risen above.

What about the remaining 5% of business organizations out there? They're another story altogether. Because they've nurtured a toxic, evil culture, they're actually a threat to the psyche of any decent employee. Companies like these honestly don't care about human beings anyway and are probably involved in some kind of nefarious moneymaking scheme.

If you ever find yourself employed by such a company, *get the heck out of there!*

In Frankl's case, however, he couldn't do that. The Nazis wouldn't let him. So he was stuck in that hell and left with only one alternative:

*He could change his mind.*

That's where genuine freedom is found anyway. The place to start changing your circumstances always starts from within.

Incredibly enough, Frankl once had an opportunity to escape with other captives, but decided against it. He felt his duty was to stay in the camp and help ease the suffering of his fellow prisoners. So he listened to his *North Star* and stayed put.

Smart decision—those who escaped were all captured and killed.

## Can't Change The Situation? Change Yourself

At some point in his captivity, Frankl realized that his current level of thinking—which was mostly negative—wasn't helping him survive. It was only contributing to feelings of hopelessness, uncertainty and insignificance.

Needless to say, depression is not a survival attribute.

The normal reaction of a person in Frankl's life-or-death situation would be to selfishly focus *on their own needs* to the exclusion of everyone else's. But Frankl got sick and tired of being sick and tired (and selfish)—a necessary shift before acting differently.

Can this be where you're at, too?

*Frankl realized that he didn't have to respond like a rat in a cage.* He was a noble human who had agency and could choose his own path.

So, from that point on, he decided to do just that.

*"When we are no longer able to change a situation we are challenged to change ourselves."*

—Viktor Frankl—

# Freedom Is *Your* Choice

*"We who lived in concentration camps can remember the men who walked through the huts comforting others, giving away their last piece of bread. They may have been few in number, but they offer sufficient proof that everything can be taken from a man but one thing: the last of human freedoms—to choose one's attitude in any given set of circumstances—to choose one's own way."*

—Viktor Frankl—

Frankl chose to unleash the human spirit of greatness within him. He ultimately liberated himself to the point where he could rise above the guards who beat him with their gun butts…starved him…even kept his family, the family he loved so much, from him.

His family meant the world to him. Not only did the Nazis take them away, they killed them all, everyone he knew and loved. Imagine everyone you love being brutally murdered?

*How about living with the uncertainty that they might still be alive?*

Frankl got to the point of believing that, "If you want to take me in front of a firing squad and shoot me, you can, but I promise you this—I've learned in my pain that my environment does not control me, my circumstances ultimately do not control me; other people do not control me. *My decisions do.*"

How about you? Does your environment control you? Or your circumstances? Or other people?

*"When you change, the world around you changes."*

—Niurka—

Or do you agree with Frankl that you can be free anytime you choose, because freedom is ultimately a state of mind?

Could anyone find meaning in a concentration camp if they so chose?

Frankl did.

## Concentration Camp Liberty

Frankl would tell you that it's entirely possible to be free in, of all places, a living hell. It was his choice and no one, not even the guards who tortured him, could take that away.

In this sense, he was free.

Physically, of course, he was still a captive. But Frankl would tell you that he had the spiritual, mental and emotional proof that a person can actually be liberated in a death camp.

*Your freedom is ultimately your choice.*
*Don't give it away to your environment,*
*circumstances or other people. You can be free*
*anytime you want. You're just one decision*
*away from revolutionizing your life.*

*The last human freedom is thought and the ability*
*to choose one's attitude and thinking at any given*
*moment!*

## What Nitpicky Little Thing Controls Your Thinking?

So who owns you?

What drives you nuts at the mere thought of it?

What are you still carrying around with you from your

youth? Does something that happened ten years ago still bother you? Is someone at work holding you hostage? Does your boss or co-worker hitch an uninvited ride home with you every night? Does your anger at trivial things—like somebody's bad driving etiquette—control your thoughts for the better part of a day?

*"Don't carry a grudge. While you're carrying
the grudge, the other guy's out dancing."*

—Buddy Hackett—

Think about it. The people you're holding a grudge over are usually oblivious of the fact. Here you are investing tons of energy in this passive anger, day after day, month after month, at this person...while they're probably home enjoying the heck out of themselves. Chances are, they haven't even given you a second thought... yet you've given them a 23$^{rd}$, a 165$^{th}$ and maybe even a 977$^{th}$ thought.

*What a waste of your time and energy!*

Another example of this is someone divorcing their spouse "to get free." Yet, afterward, they remain hopelessly captive to the former mate. They can leave their spouse...*they just can't leave them alone.*

I love showing people how to get all the freedom they want in marriage, enough so they'd never, ever think of divorce again.

## How Would Viktor Frankl Live A Day In *Your* Life?

Now that you know a little something about Frankl— and I still advise you to read his life-changing book,

*Man's Search for Meaning*—how do you think he'd go about living *one of your days*?

Hmmm...

Well, okay, he wakes up in the morning, and what's the first thing he thinks of? No, not that he hates his job and has to drag himself through another weary, dreary day.

Frankl definitely doesn't like thinking that way. So he doesn't.

What he does think about is that he has another remarkable day...and all the freedom in the world to think anything he wants...and that today just may be an important day of discovery and opportunity.

Not to get too Pollyanna-ish on you, but Frankl probably wouldn't be mired in the same negativity you often find yourself stuck in simply because he would have decided against that sort of thing long ago.

Okay, so he gets to your workplace with that same nagging, griping boss who's on your case morning until night, the same *zero* upward mobility, and the same fellow workers who couldn't give a crap about the quality of products and services your company puts out.

What does he do? Frankl would take an objective look around. This isn't a look born of desperation or fear, mind you, but of accurate observation and intelligent assessment.

And he does this cheerfully, *because that's how he likes to feel.*

Right away your boss launches into him. Does that get to him as much as it does you? Nahhh. Frankl's far too resilient for that. If Nazi brutality in a concentration camp couldn't break him, do you think your boss, as nasty as he is, would even be a blip on his screen?

Frankl would just do the work required of him to the best of his ability...but he'd be doing something else at the same time. Based on his quick assessment of the job, he'd consider whether or not he'd be happier at another job, a less toxic place with more positive, conscientious co-workers surrounding him, and more opportunity to express the talents he knows he possesses.

On the other hand, he would also remember that the grass isn't always greener somewhere else—that sometimes the problems we run away from are the same ones we run right back into. So he might choose to stay put for the time being. And since there are no armed guards forcing him to leave or stay at the job, he's free to do whatever he wants.

He revels in that freedom.

While he's deciding what to do, he works hard and is very supportive of your co-workers, helping them out as much as he can.

Because that's what makes him the happiest...and Frankl enjoys making himself happy.

## Frankl After Work

The workday over, Frankl returns home, humming.

But, of course, there's that nagging spouse and those out-of-control kids of yours.

Frankl, however, doesn't want to be saddled with somebody else's negativity, so he chooses to stay on the positive side (although your spouse can get pretty doom-and-gloom-ish).

But that doesn't faze him in the least. He decides to make his optimism *bulletproof.*

Soon the atmosphere in the household lightens up. Even the kids seem a bit more responsive and obedient.

Frankl knows that whatever attitude he chooses can be quite contagious.

After an upbeat meal, and some time spent with the family, he gets on the Internet to start his search for a better job. He knows that it might not happen overnight, but he also knows, with persistent effort, he'll eventually find what he's looking for.

Meanwhile, he'll thoroughly enjoy his time searching and working at your job.

Because that's Frankl.

## How You Focus Your Mind

Does the foregoing mean anything to you?

Can you see how our attitudes *do not have to be the result of what happens to us during the day?* Instead of always being *reactive*, you have the freedom of *first determining the attitude you want* then letting everything in your day flow from there?

Ever hear of Napoleon Hill? Author of *Think and Grow Rich*, one of the best-selling books of all time? If so, do you recall the expression, *"What the mind of man can conceive and believe, it can achieve"*?

Well, this pioneer of positive thinking also said something else.

*"The one and only thing over which you have complete and total control is how you focus your own mind."*

*"Luckily, this determines everything else."*

Wow.

If the last few pages have taught you anything it should be that you have far more control over your life than you probably thought. The titanic, gigantic obstacle illusion you've been operating under, up to this point, is that you're absolutely powerless to control your life.

That you can never really grab hold of *The Helm*.

Nothing could be further from the truth.

## Focus Is The Key

Note, Napoleon Hill said, "The one and only thing over which you have complete and total control is how you FOCUS your own mind."

*So when was the last time you really focused on a personal matter on your own time?*

When was the last time, for example, you decided to spend an hour each day, for two whole weeks, actively focusing on finding a solution to a particular challenge of yours?

It's funny but if your boss "ordered" you to spend an hour each day for the next couple of weeks looking for a solution to a corporate problem, you wouldn't think twice about it, right (other than to maybe grumble a bit)?

Yet people rarely invest that kind of time and focus *on their own problems*.

Here's another question: When was the last time you stayed focused enough to pray or meditate for, say, seven straight days for specific direction on a problem?

How about 14 straight days?

Or have you ever been focused enough to try *fasting* for a couple of days while you searched and prayed for an answer?

Wow. Fasting. Now *that's* focus and intensity…the kind that hits you right in the belly…and, amazingly enough, often gets results.

**PRACTICAL TIP:** Okay, right now, you probably have some issues you want to resolve, some new direction you want to take. So here's the challenge: Take the next three days and spend a half-hour to an hour just focusing on finding the answers. Now here's what this time is not: It's not TV time, nap time, video game time, exercise time or reading time. Remember when we did the half-hour reflection exercise back in Chapter 2? Well, this is a *practical application of your growing ability to reflect*. As before, go someplace quiet and just think about your challenge. *Exercise your ability to reflect*. Stretch your contemplative muscles.

STAY FOCUSED THE WHOLE TIME.

*Then* see if you can repeat that for three straight days.

*If you do,* I *guarantee* you one thing: You will gain new insights into what you need to do, if not find outright answers to your challenge.

## What You Can Control ...And What You Can't

In Frankl's case, he wrestled back control of his attitude and that gave him the key to surviving an intolerable situation.

But make no mistake, Frankl was in physical bondage. If he went about his day whistling, skipping and telling himself he was on a glorious sunny beach instead of a hideous death camp, he would have deluded himself big time.

And that would have eventually been a formula for insanity.

Trying to control things you really can't is like trying to teach a penguin to fly. Yes, penguins do have wings and, yes, penguins technically are birds, but the inescapable truth is, they *can't* fly. That's the reality no matter how much you wish it were otherwise, no matter how much time you spent training that penguin to get airborne.

In the end, you and the penguin would be disappointed.

Actually the penguin wouldn't be disappointed at all. It knows it can't fly and is perfectly okay with that. It concerns itself with other penguin issues.

Along these lines, I absolutely love Reinhold Niebuhr's "Serenity Prayer."

*"God, give us grace to accept with serenity the things that cannot be changed, courage to change the things that should be changed, and the wisdom to distinguish the one from the other."*

With apologies to Niebuhr, here's an addition to the prayer you might appreciate:

> *"God, give me the grace to accept the people I cannot change, the courage to change the one I can, and the wisdom to know that that person is me."*

Like Viktor Frankl exhibited and Napoleon Hill wrote, the one and only thing you truly can control is *your attitude and thinking*. But, in the end, that can be enough.

Frankl discussed the idea that...

> *"...there comes a time in your life when you must force yourself to stop entertaining the trivial (the things you can't control)—not to say that they*

*"Figure out what you're passionate about.
If you're not passionate about something,
go find it. We do not need more unengaged
boring people to inhabit this planet."*

—Ben Heppner—

*are not important, but simply out of your span of control—and enter into the realm of the significant (the things you can control—yourself)."*

## Unrealistic Thinking And Self-Sabotage

Unrealistic/unhealthy expectations are at the center of all mental illusions. They form when you fail to take a good, honest look at your life. They're what happen when you regard the unattainable as obtainable...and the obtainable as unattainable.

Now, granted, as with Frankl's incredible triumph in the concentration camp, impossible things can and do happen whenever remarkable people focus and apply themselves over a sufficient period of time. So it doesn't make sense to set your sights too low.

But neither does it make sense to set your sights unrealistically high. You could, for example, set the goal to try out and make the *Utah Jazz* this season as an unathletic, overweight guy in his mid-30s...when such a thing really *does* border on the impossible. Kind of like that flying penguin.

Of course, sometimes people will set unrealistic goals *on purpose* as their way of sabotaging themselves.

See, they've never really assembled the faith necessary to accomplish anything great in the first place, so they just set these vague, ridiculous goals—something that may sound good at parties—then expend a token, mediocre effort, if that, toward attaining them.

Don't be one of these folks.

Take a good, unvarnished look at your life, at the things that are realistically (and, alright, maybe *a tad* unrealistically) achievable, then set an earnest daily plan to reach them.

Peter Drucker said that…"*Plans are only good intentions unless they immediately degenerate into hard work.*" So don't just plan, *work*.

When Frankl was in the death camp, he first came to terms with his dismal reality. That was his first admittedly brutal step, given the circumstances. After that, he was able to choose a course of action that gave him his best chance at survival. If he never did that, if he had lived in denial, his story probably would have died along with him in the camp.

*Taking The Helm*, whether you're in a tiny work cubicle, a crowded suburb or a death camp, can lead to your liberation.

## So How Bad Do You Want It?

Frankl resolved, in the marrow of his soul, that he was absolutely, positively going to gain control of his life and get free while inside that concentration camp. Have you ever been *that* determined? *That* passionate? It's a "burn the boats and charge the beach, I'm 100% committed to conquering" kind of attitude.

Notice this isn't a "50%, 60% or 70% committed to conquering" kind of attitude?

That percentage, while it may accomplish *something*, won't get you where you want to be.

**This is a 100% commitment**.

*Is there anything you're willing to commit 100% of yourself to accomplish right now?*

*"Man does not simply exist, but always decides what his existence will be, what he will become in the next moment."*

—Viktor Frankl—

*"There is something in every one of you that waits and listens for the sound of the genuine in yourself. It is the only true guide you will ever have. And if you cannot hear it, you will all of your life spend your days on the ends of strings that somebody else pulls."*

—Howard Thurman—

# Chapter 10

# THE FOUR SECRETS

*How to absolutely, positively, without a doubt gain control of your life. How loud can you listen?*

A number of years ago, while a kid in Virginia, I had what I now realize was the voice of my *North Star* warning me to check the front tire of my bike. But being too busy at the moment, unfortunately, I blew the prompting off.

Then the prompting returned. Two more times, in fact.

And two more times I blew it off.

A couple of days later, while riding to a skateboard shop, I did a bunny hop into the parking lot. The funny thing was, though, my front tire didn't join me. It came right off in mid-air! The now wheel-less forks of my bike stabbed the asphalt, instantly arresting my momentum and hurling me over my handlebars at what felt like light speed.

My shirt and pants were ripped up, and I got "road rashed" pretty well. A nearby group of boarders cheered me on, thinking I had done it deliberately, and asked me to do it again. I didn't feel in any mood to oblige.

## Can You Hear It?

Later, reflecting on this, I realized I had once again ignored the voice of my *North Star*.

For maybe the first time in my life, I knew I needed to be a better listener.

Frankl had a strong connection to his *North Star*, one he not only understood but wasn't afraid to act on. It was constantly "calling" him to a greater purpose. Think of the consequences if he hadn't listened?

Ultimately your *North Star* will lead you to your *Lighthouse* and the creation of miracles in your life, too.

*"Opportunities to find deeper powers within ourselves come when life seems most challenging."*

—Joseph Campbell—

## When Was The Last Time You Heard The Voice?

Remember Frankl's chance to join an escape attempt? His *North Star* saved his life by warning him against it.

How connected to your *North Star* are you? When was the last time you *recognized, listened* to and *acted on* its whisperings?

Just because you haven't done so in a long time— *listened for your North Star*—doesn't mean that its enlightened support is gone for good. It's much like an old radio station you used to listen to but no longer do. Assuming it's not on the air anymore just because you haven't been listening is a false assumption.

As mentioned before, it can be something of an art to decipher the voice of your *North Star*, but you can start right this moment to improve your connection. And one of the biggest things you can do is reduce the "interference."

**PRACTICAL TIP:** Interference? That's the almost constant barrage of media impacting our thinking, our lives today. Don't think it impacts you? Okay, try this: If you have an iPod or something like it, put on those earbuds and crank up the music. Next, have your spouse or friend read the instructions to, say, some new kitchen gadget you just bought.

How many of those instructions did you actually hear? Did you get the whole idea, more or less? Or just a word here or there?

Or nada?

That's effectively what it's like trying to listen to your *North Star* in the sea of sound we typically live in. It's a pretty hard thing to do.

We've talked about taking *silent moment breaks* several times through this book. If you can practice taking meaningful time-outs, you'll greatly increase your concentration and improve your chances of picking up those indispensable truths your *North Star* is patiently trying to tell you.

## Like A Peanut Butter
## And Chocolate Collision

Life has a way of preparing you to *Take Life by the Helm*. The truth is, life is preparing you, through all your tough challenges, to take the next steps in becoming your very best self.

Your challenges, the pain you grow through, are fabulous instructors for liberation and growth, maybe the best you'll ever have.

How Viktor Frankl was able to hear the voice of his *North Star* amid the unspeakable cruelty and suffering of the camp, I'll never know.

BUT, THE POINT IS, HE DID IT...AND SO CAN YOU!

When you combine your challenges with the voice of your *North Star*, meaning and miracles are sure to follow.

Like that old TV commercial where two delivery trucks collide and chocolate is accidentally shoved into peanut butter to create one amazing taste, you must have both your challenges and the voice of your *North Star* present to fulfill your greatest potential.

Otherwise you may forever remain a victim of your obstacle illusions.

## Take Life By The Helm *Primer*

*Once fixed on a meaningful course the human spirit is unstoppable and can rise above anything. Even death.*

Below is a summary of what I believe was the foundation for Frankl's taking *The Helm:*

1) **Discontent.** This is the first step in doing something different. You know that parachute that keeps dragging you backward as you drive to work? Or that concrete block you feel in your belly after

doing your housework and looking out over the dead grass in your backyard? Or that fingernails-on-the-chalkboard panic you have Sunday night when you think about the coming week? *That's discontent.* Is it there for a reason? You bet. It's there to urge you to try something different, something more satisfying. Pay attention to it.

2) **Clarity.** To reach a goal, it needs to be crystal clear. If it's ambiguous or poorly defined, good luck with it. Something like that will be hard for your brain to properly pinpoint and stay focused on. So...become 100% clear on exactly what it is you want to do. Nothing wavering.

3) **Hope.** Let's face it, hope is the fuel of miracles. No hope, no miracles. So keep your flame of hope burning brightly, no matter what. Frankl would tell you that he certainly witnessed a lot of suffering, but it was never enough to kill the hope inside. A family counselor once said that it's when a person never sees a light at the end of the tunnel and can only anticipate more of the same desperate circumstances ahead that he or she is prone to start giving up, mentally, spiritually and physically. So hope truly is a valuable commodity...one that can actually keep you alive.

4) **New Normals.** When the road gets rocky, and it inevitably will, you can do one of two things: You can turn back to where it's familiar and safe or you can grit your teeth, tighten your gut and keep going. *Often, going on means moving into uncharted* **territory, a place you've never been before, making efforts you've never made before. All of this will likely be unfamiliar...and that's entirely okay!** When you rise to greatness, you establish "new normals" in your life.

5) **Listen.** As I talked about before, **listen to your North Star for inspiration and direction no matter how much clutter and clatter surrounds you**. This is a key step, but I'm not going to sugarcoat it for you—it's something you'll have to practice. You've got to get good at listening to the hushed inspiration that finds its way to you.

6) **Understand.** Burn this in your brain: **There's a direct connection between your thoughts and your actions**. Ralph Waldo Emerson said, "Every action has an ancestor of a thought." Does that mean you'll want to start gaining better control over your thinking? Is this book written in English? **YES!**

7) **Love.** Can't you just hear a wild Tina Turner singing, "What's love got to do with it?" Well, what does love have to do with going through great trials? Plenty, in fact. Love is inspiration, a great motivator, and can even be the nucleus of your willpower. Frankl thought intently about his wife, about her qualities, the way she looked, the way she felt, everything. That love ultimately fueled his victory.

## Staying Power

The weight of my son's health scare, our house-building nightmare plus my crazy work situation all made me realize it was time for a change. The foundation had certainly been laid, and I was 100% committed to following through.

The instant I heard Frankl tell me, in his own words, that he "took life by the helm," I was forever changed. His words pierced my very being to the soul. In short...

*I got it.*

Does that mean I stayed unwavering on that new road from that point on? *C'mon.* But I knew I had made a breakthrough and knew I would do everything in my power to take advantage of it.

"Doug," I said to myself (in a fatherly kind of voice), "for the first time in your life, you can be in control. Don't give this away. Don't ever give it away again. It's your choice. Don't let anyone or anything dictate your attitude or actions again. Get free and stay there. Because if ever there was a time when your little boy needed you, it's right now. If ever there was a time when your wife needed you, it's right now. And if ever there was a time when your employees needed you, it's right now."

So how about you? Are you in control?

Or do you just tell yourself that you are?

## The Soundtrack To Your New Life

Life can be meaningful and amazing right this moment if you want it to be. And I do mean, right now.

And right now.

And right now.

You can take all the "right now" moments in your life and make them memorable and beautiful if you want.

Maybe the only thing missing is, in fact, a soundtrack. You know...the music behind the great movies?

Maybe like something John Williams would compose?

---

PRACTICAL TIP: *Well, why not get a soundtrack to your new life?* It could be a great theme, a great symbol, something to listen to when you need to be energized.

Is there a movie soundtrack you particularly like? Something that gives you the chills whenever you hear it? You say you don't know? Well, if you have *iTunes* or something like it, you can audition all the soundtracks you like for that special one.

Don't discount such a thing. Music has a profound impact on the human soul. Your soundtrack can be just the emotional fuel you need to power you on your journey.

## Perception Really Is Greater Than Reality

I think we've established that your personal freedom *is ultimately determined by the way you think*. It's a choice you constantly make.

The old adage that perception is greater (or more meaningful) than reality is indeed a fact.

Example, what's more beautiful than a sunrise or sunset? On my business card I have a picture of the sun over the ocean. It could be a sunrise. Or a sunset. Whatever the holder of the business card perceives it to be, it is.

Like sunrises better than sunsets? Well, there you go. Like it better the other way around? There you go again.

It's your choice. No one will ever argue with you about what my business cards are or aren't.

I've learned from sad experience never to try to argue with someone over their "realities." It's futile. I must admit though, on occasion, I've tried changing my wife's mind to something more closely resembling mine. And she always catches on and quickly reminds me that the last real decision I made was to marry her.

She's gotten all the rest since.

## Four Secrets To Absolutely, Positively Taking Control Of Your Life!

As I've studied Viktor Frankl, my own life experiences, the lives of thousands of clients I've worked with, and the latest peak performance research, four basic themes keep popping up in regards to *Taking Life by The Helm*.

They are: *Stop and Drop Anchor, Get Your Bearings, Ignore Negative Thinking, Chart Your Course/Set Sail for Miracles*. We've gone over some of these principles earlier, but let's put a finer point on them now.

# *Secret #1: Stop And Drop Anchor*

And this means? *Take ownership of your situation!*

Don't blame anyone or anything, play the "what if" game, or rationalize yourself silly. Instead, *own it!* This is *your* problem, *your* situation, and if you didn't exactly get yourself into it, it's now your job *to get yourself out of it*. So, with all due respect, own it.

Frankl didn't volunteer to get thrown into a prison camp. But it wasn't until he decided that how he felt and acted *was entirely in his own hands* that things finally began to change. He knew he couldn't possibly solve a problem until he made it his own. Until he owned it, it would just remain something nasty someone did to him, a problem he had zero control over.

*"You are the only person alive who has sole custody of your life...Your entire life...Not just the life of your mind, but the life of your heart. Not just your bank account, but your soul."*

—Anna Quindlen—

> **PRACTICAL TIP:** As part of taking 100% ownership, write down the event that's causing you the most stress. Write it in gritty detail. Be as brutally honest as you can. Don't censor your thoughts. List the negative feelings you're experiencing. How you see the situation. How unfair it all is. How uncertain or out-of-control you feel.
>
> Next write what you want to happen, what you believe the outcome should be. What needs to take place to give your situation a happy ending.
>
> Get it all down on paper. Reduced to paper and ink, it all becomes rather matter-of-fact. And, once you see it in that way, the illusions and solutions may become more apparent.

# Secret #2:
# Get Your Bearings

Check your number one navigational instrument—*your emotions*—to see if you're off course. What are your emotions telling you?

Probably, among other things, that you are the greatest authority on yourself.

Think about it. You know exactly when you're feeling positive about something...and when you're feeling doubtful, suspicious or mostly "off."

So your feelings serve as your own personal Geiger counter. Run them by your situation and see if they start "clicking."

*"Thought is cause: experience is effect. If you don't like the effects in your life, you have to change the nature of your thinking."*

—Marianne Williamson—

Next check out your thoughts. How do you *act* when you think about your situation or challenge? How do you *treat yourself and others* when you're thinking of these things? Remember that whatever thoughts you're thinking right now, *you're attracting more of the same.* Kind of like the way heat attracts a heat-seeking missile.

Your brain will attract whatever reality you want it to.

Are your present thoughts propelling you to greatness? Or leading you to take your hands off *The Helm*?

File this under awareness and the beginning of progress. Frankl became aware that his thoughts would ultimately bring him life or death. He had to stay on high alert to detect angry, depressive and hopeless thoughts and nip them in the bud.

His feelings helped him stay on top of that.

In a death camp, thinking is serious business. A matter of life and death, actually. In the same vein, your thoughts will either build or kill off your dreams.

---

**PRACTICAL TIP:** Still have that piece of paper? Let's see if we can identify a correlation here. On any given day, you probably have some powerful feelings, right? Anger, envy, sadness, lust? Well, write them down on the left side of the paper as you feel them (or can remember them). Okay? Now, on the right side of the paper, write down the thoughts you often get that correlate with those feelings.

See the cause-and-effect thing you've got going on here?

*"You've done it before and you can do it now. See the positive possibilities. Redirect the substantial energy of your frustration and turn it into positive, effective, unstoppable determination."*

—Ralph Marston—

# Secret #3:
# Consult Your North Star To Overcome Negative Thinking

If you were to consult your *North Star*, what would it say about your negative thinking? What thoughts would it advise you to think instead?

Could you suddenly adopt a positive frame of mind? You may be surprised. Negative patterns of thought can be pretty stubborn things.

Let's say you're walking through the mall and see something that kicks off a negative thought.

A frustratingly familiar negative thought.

There you are, trying to be in the here-and-now, and you're suddenly enveloped by this negative canopy you've, sad to say, come to know only too well.

What do you do?

Well, first off, you need to be aware of it, just like Frankl had to be. And that's not always easy to do. Sometimes, to the unexamined life, negative thoughts can fly under the radar. They can just seem like another permanent fixture of the daily grind. But negative thoughts are never that. They simply don't belong.

But you first have to see 'em.

And after that, you need to get past them. So what's your best technique for doing that?

**PRACTICAL TIP:** This is an interesting problem, one that, surprisingly enough, is also pretty common. And a telltale sign of this *thought-struggle* is—ready for it?—*breathing.*

According to anecdotal reports, people have noted that, whenever negative thoughts arise, they find their breathing pattern a bit altered. Some found that they tended to actually *hold their breath* more when preoccupied with an uninvited negative thought.

So here's the technique: *Just breathe.* You know…like the Faith Hill song? Whenever a negative thought arises, ignore it and just concentrate on your breathing. Keep it going deeply and rhythmically.

After a short time, the thought will evaporate, and you'll return to a nice, neutral state of awareness.

Which is exactly where you want to be.

## Two Ideas In Dealing With Obstacle Illusions

Can you deal with obstacle illusions, the kind that would have surely killed Frankl had he been content to co-exist with them?

Sure thing.

Here's the first idea:

> **PRACTICAL TIP:** It's an affirmation actually,
> something to say when your old illusions threaten to
> drag you back into the mire.
>
> "I am alive for a reason, to contribute and service
> others. I am not on this Earth to feel inferior, to play
> it small and push my wants and needs under the
> carpet. I have a high opinion of myself, and I love
> others. I matter!"

And the second idea?

Don't try to change things that are literally unchangeable (remember the penguin). The modification in your thinking here is to *simply decide to accept reality.*

Yeah, I know, there's a balance to all this. You want to set your sights high, but not unrealistically high. You want to accept realities but not get mired in mediocrity. It can get confusing. With time and effort, though, I promise you'll get the hang of it.

To give you an example, let's say that after a year you're still upset about some corporate restructuring and remain passively aggressive with your boss. Remember the way the old hippies used to protest? They'd lay down and have to be dragged out of the way. Well, you're kind of doing that now (except you're probably not lying down on the corporate carpeting). You resist everything, whether consciously or subconsciously.

But where is that going to get you, besides the unemployment line?

Think about it. The restructuring is done, the new employees are in place and there you are, still tapping away on your computer with that sullen, negative look on your face. Is pouting going to change anything? No siree, Bob. So either *own* the restructuring and *adjust* your attitude...or *leave*.

Just don't pout.

No sense torturing yourself by taking some futile, pain-filled, middle-of-the-road course. Or poisoning everyone around you, including your co-workers, clients and loved ones.

Another sadder, more personal example is when a relationship ends and a man or woman struggles to accept the fact. Although their former spouse may have moved on, may have even re-married by then, the one left behind continues to harbor hopes that they'll someday be reunited.

By that time, though, it's everlastingly too late.

The only positive change you can make from that point on *is to prepare yourself for a future relationship*, one that will prove successful this time. Sure, the self-examination can be brutal. It can take painful honesty to admit your own weaknesses and identify the negativity that helped squash the first relationship.

But self-examination is a very useful thing to do, especially if you want to enjoy marital bliss one sweet day.

## Negativity Takes Up Valuable Energy

We all get angry over things that have happened to us.

We each carry a résumé of disappointments, tragedies and inequities. Not all of us, though, keep those things *alive* inside.

Believe it or not, *it takes lots of energy to maintain anger and disappointment in our minds and bodies.*

Quite a bit of it, actually. Every time you think a thought, a bit of electrical energy is discharged. So if you decide to heft a heavy burden of negative emotions from the past, it can consume a disturbing amount of your daily ration of energy. Think of it as trying to run a hundred-yard dash...*while dragging a twenty-pound dumbbell behind you.*

Or sailing...while dragging an anchor.

Believe me, you just don't have that kind of energy to waste.

I remember watching a pro basketball game where the guard got embarrassed. He was stripped of the ball then slam-dunked on. Instead of just moving on and playing better, he seemed to spend the rest of the time trying to get back at his opponent (rather than win the game). Needless to say, it affected his performance, blunted his team's effort, and the team, to no one's surprise, lost.

It would have been so much better had he just put the embarrassment behind him and moved on with his game, playing the best he could from that point on (revenge, after all, is a plate best served up cold).

But he just couldn't do it on that day.

Bad things happen in life. It's so much better if you can make peace with them and move on from there. For one reason, *you'll save so much energy!*

Here's another affirmation:

> *"I'm not your puppet who reacts when you pull my strings. You don't own me or control me. My DECISIONS DO! I'm in control of my life from here on. I no longer give you the power to enslave me. My life is created one decision at a time."*

## The Difference Between A Fact And A Problem

There's a difference between a "fact" and a "problem."

A fact is a statement of truth—the sky is blue, the ground is hard, the temperature is cold.

A problem may or may not be an accurate assessment of a situation...but it does come with a solution. *I'm cold, I'm hungry, I'm wet.* The solution here would obviously be, *find warmth, find food, find dry clothes.*

You *accept* facts. You look to *solve* problems. You run into trouble when you get the two confused—when you try to solve facts and accept problems. This is a no-win game, something akin to bashing your head against the wall.

You also run into trouble when you don't get your facts straight for the simple reason that you haven't done enough research. That's how we build great big mental illusions.

We act—or fail to act—on *bad information.*

Your judgment is only as good as the knowledge you possess.

Mental illusions that spring up from bad information are much like those circus funhouse mirrors. The image in the mirror bears a faint resemblance to reality, but that's about it (thank goodness).

The "fact" was that Frankl was in a concentration camp... but he accurately identified the "problem" as being his thinking. Thought is a choice, something that can be changed and resolved.

When you get stuck in negative thinking, stop and connect with your *North Star.* Ask for help to refute

and replace that destructive thinking. Don't worry...
your *North Star* will never be a supporter of negative
thinking. It'll never go over to the dark side.

The sometimes disturbing reality is, most problems
reside in the mind.

# Secret #4:
# Chart Your Course,
# Set Sail For Miracles

Ask yourself this simple question, "What do I really
want to have happen in my life?"

Next, identify the one baby step you can take today to
help you get there. Often it will mean doing the one
thing you don't feel like doing, the one thing you can't
do, the one thing you don't know how to do or that is
incredibly boring.

*The one thing that seems impossible.*

Miracles come in all shapes and sizes. From overcoming
addiction to getting in great shape.

You'll know a miracle is happening when you catch
yourself thinking, feeling or acting in a way you
once thought was impossible. But now *it happens
almost effortlessly.*

When it does, it will undoubtedly take you by surprise,
so be on the lookout for your miracle.

Getting back to those baby steps, can you think of one
right now that will set you on a course to miracles?

## Loving The Unlovable

So what's Frankl's next secret?

*"There are only two ways to live your life. One is as though nothing is a miracle. The other is as if everything is."*

—Albert Einstein—

*How about loving the unlovable?*

Huh?

Loving the unlovable means doing just that: Deciding to do what 99% of people never, ever do—learning to love what others hate.

For instance?

- Is there someone lots of folks can't stand, someone who used to drive you crazy? *Decide today that you'll be the one who now gets along famously with that person.*

- Do you have a boss few employees tolerate? *Decide that you'll be the one who, through your patience and effort (and not by kissing up), makes it work.*

- Is there a situation no one wants to touch? *Decide that you'll be the one who conquers it.*

Get the idea? The one who conquers a challenge is often the one who does what no one else wants to do...the one who takes on the seemingly impossible.

There's another word for this kind of person.

*Leader.*

A word on miracles: In therapy people often come seeking some sort of miracle. They're stuck hoping for a breakthrough. I pay particular attention whenever a client starts saying things like, "I can't do that...there's no way...I don't feel like doing that." The reason I listen carefully is that these are the exact kinds of statements that lead to miracles. Miracles are found in the things you don't want to do, or that seem impossible, yet your *North Star* nudges you to engage them anyway.

I invite you to be on the lookout for opportunities found only in the seemingly impossible.

Frankl was a leader in the camp because he did just that. He went beyond himself and his own personal needs to support those he felt were in *greater* need. He developed an almost surreal selflessness and graciousness.

In so doing, he advanced his own soul way beyond normal human boundaries and became an incredible inspiration, both in the camps and after he was liberated from them.

By loving the unlovable, he fulfilled the measure of his creation and became the Frankl his Creator always knew he was capable of being.

Maybe this is how you'll fulfill the measure of your creation, too.

Is there a similar challenge looming ahead of you? A door you can take that no one else wants to chance? An unlovable person, place or thing that you can turn around by investing your own love?

The funny thing is, after loving the unlovable for a while, *you'll find that you truly do love that person or thing* and will be sad and miss them whenever you two eventually part.

## Which Comes First? Motivation Or Action?

Maybe this is a chicken-or-the-egg issue, I don't know.

If pushed, most folks would probably say motivation comes first. After all, you need some impetuous energy to actually drive yourself to take the first few steps, don't you?

I'm firmly in the other camp.

Some folks have little to no motivation, yet struggle ahead in a particular direction anyway. Then they bump into motivation along the way.

Were you ever driven to buy a piece of exercise equipment...only to have it become a dust collector? The problem was, you had enough motivation to buy the equipment but no established exercise habit to actually take advantage of it. That's what I mean by action coming ahead of motivation.

Motivation alone isn't always enough.

That was my story with the paper route I did as a kid. Goodness knows I sure didn't want to do it at first. But it got easier the more I did it, especially as I began enjoying the money it made me. I became more motivated to get out there and do it every single day.

I remember a friend who played football in high school. He had a tough coach who was unsympathetic with an injury he got almost on day one, and my buddy suddenly found himself with zero motivation to continue with the team. All he could do, at that point, was not quit. That was all he had at the moment.

*Just don't quit.*

He couldn't see any reason to go on but was simply determined not to leave the team. Time passed, and he squeaked through those motivation-less days and started first tolerating then enjoying the coach and his tough brand of football...which was a really good thing because he was ultimately to become the captain of that soon-to-be championship team.

Act first. If the motivation's not there, it will follow.

## I Don't Feel Like Being A Prison Camp Hero Today

I'm sure Frankl didn't always feel like serving those who were sick and exhausted, particularly when he was sick and exhausted himself. We simply can't imagine

> *"If a man is called to be a street sweeper, he should sweep streets even as Michelangelo painted, or Beethoven composed music, or Shakespeare wrote poetry. He should sweep streets so well that all the hosts of Heaven and Earth will pause to say, 'Here lived a great street sweeper who did his job well!'"*

—Martin Luther King Jr.—

the circumstances of cold, squalor, hunger and brutality he faced on a daily basis.

But he understood this important truth:

*Motivation almost always arrives after you've acted. Not before.*

In your life, when have you gotten the most excited about something? When you were looking at it from the outside and really knew next to nothing about it? Or from the inside, after you got over the hard initiatory phase and could now see the real possibilities?

The latter, right? That's because this is the glorious "I-now-know-I-can-do-it" phase.

Is there something you'd like to try but can't seem to muster the necessary effort? True, this is always the hardest part...but if you can just gather yourself enough to give it a good try for a reasonable amount of time, you may find your motivational levels rising right along with your skill and endurance.

And that's what will sustain you—exactly as it has sustained countless people of merit—on your road to greatness.

If Frankl sat around waiting to be motivated, he would have waited right up until the moment he died. Which, in that camp, wouldn't have taken very long. There's no right time or way to take that first momentous step.

The key is just taking it.

Look to your *North Star* for guidance here. Then, whatever you decide to do, go all out and don't look back.

## 300-Pound Lineman Love

"All you need is love."

That was, of course, from Beatle John Lennon.

Love really is all *you* need. It's the shorthand of success, the best advice you could get in one little word.

No, this doesn't mean that if you're this big 300-pound former college lineman you now need to blow kisses and skip through fields of daisies absolutely adoring everything in sight.

That wouldn't work for you anyway.

But loving something—a person, a job, a challenge, anything—has more to do with the *intensity and passion* of your involvement than anything else.

"I love engineering." "I love plowing snow." "I love helping people." "I love writing stories."

Love means not being middle-of-the-road. If you love something, *you're into it*. With both feet. With all of the resources the good Lord has invested in you.

So loving something is a good thing...whether you're a 300-pound lineman, a 100-pound ballerina or somebody in between.

## *Your* Problem?

It's funny but, sometimes, we can get a little too close to our problems.

And a little too familiar. They become "ours." We talk about them in possessive terms. *My tumor, my arthritis, my heart trouble, my cancer, my financial problems.* The way we refer to them, you'd think they were family members, part of a long-term relationship.

And so they are.

Which isn't smart thinking. Yes, the problems we're given are not there to destroy us. They're there to build us into better people than we already are.

Problems are opportunities, no more, no less.

*But, for the most part, we were never intended to be saddled with them forever.*

They exist at a specific time and place to help us improve in that specific time and place. Once we learn from them, grow as much as we can from them, endure and overcome them, we have the privilege of doing something few actually do.

We can let them go.

How do you do that exactly? There's actually a nice, little ceremony.

---

**PRACTICAL TIP:** Here's what a friend once told me:

"Go to the supermarket and buy one of those helium balloons you always see bobbing around in there. On a clear day in your backyard, and using a felt marker, write your particular issue right on the balloon. Be as specific as you can."

"Next, sum up the situation aloud and say that it's time for you to move on. Say goodbye, and then, with scissors, cut the string holding the balloon."

"Watch the balloon rise into the heavens as long as you can. Watch it getting smaller and smaller until it's this insignificant little dot. When you can't see it anymore, nod farewell, go back in the house and get on with your life."

"Making this goodbye a formal ceremony, making it very visual, symbolic and dramatic, can go a long way in helping you ultimately retire this issue to a healthy place in your past."

---

By the way, in case I need to mention it, from this point on, please don't refer to any problem that comes your way as "*my* problem."

Refer to it as "*the* problem."

Subtle but important difference.

## Love Anyway

We talked about love?

The fact is, love is the greatest indicator that you're at *The Helm*. Sounds crazy, doesn't it...but being at *The Helm* really is an emotional state of heart. Love lets you see your big picture (versus your life in the claustrophobic shadows).

Frankl was ultimately liberated by love.

---

> *"People are unreasonable, illogical and self-centered. Love them anyway. If you do good, people will accuse you of selfish ulterior motives. Do good anyway. If you are successful, you will win false friends and true enemies. Succeed anyway. Honesty and frankness make you vulnerable. Be honest and frank anyway."*
>
> —Dr. Kent Keith—

---

In short? Simply love and embrace your trials and challenges. In them, you'll find growth and freedom. Without them, *you wouldn't be where you are today*.

One more time: There are no problems in life, only opportunities for growth and love.

So...the next time you see someone who can get under

your skin, silently thank the person for teaching you how to take *The Helm*.

## An Invitation

**PRACTICAL TIP:** Are you ready to live an amazing life? Then you're ready to apply Frankl's Four Secrets.

For starters, I invite you to identify an obstacle illusion you may currently have and run it through the above Four Secrets. See how that can help.

In fact, with practice, you can make the Four Secrets your "screening habit," your way of filtering illusions out of your life. Stick these four steps on the mirror to remind you, put them on 3x5 cards, put them on a screen saver, on your phone, PDA, computer.

*Write them in your heart.*

I cannot put into words the miracles I've seen when people applied these powerful steps. Don't expect perfection, just do your best, screw up, get over it and keep going.

The goal is to practice using them until they become a part of who you are.

These secrets work. Absolutely. Positively. Without a doubt.

*"This is the true joy in life, the being used for a purpose recognized by yourself as a mighty one; the being thoroughly worn out before you are thrown on the scrap heap; the being a force of nature instead of a feverish selfish little clod of ailments and grievances complaining that the world will not dedicate itself to making you happy."*

—George Bernard Shaw—

# Chapter 11

# NOW WHERE DID I PUT MY PURPOSE?

A few years back I worked with a client who had given up on her dream of being a successful businesswoman, spouse and loving mother. So completely had she given up, in fact, that she contemplated disappearing from society altogether.

She was just going to drive far away and start over in some place new.

The lady was angry at the world, at how her best attempts to make life successful simply fizzled. At work, her team was stagnant, devoid of leadership. At home, her family avoided her caustic, sarcastic attitude.

Inside she was numb.

So she decided to quit trying...until she had a conversation with her grandma.

She described her granny as the kind every kid dreamed of. Kind and loving yet honest and insightful when she needed to be. She told me, "Granny delivered a message I so desperately needed. I remember we were sitting on her porch, by her swimming pool, in those old green-colored metal lawn chairs. I told her how empty I was feeling. She listened and asked a few questions—she had this uncanny way of entering my world without ever judging me. It was one of the safest environments I have ever been in."

"After spilling my heart, I asked her what she thought. She said only one sentence:

'Honey, I've come to understand that this life is not so much about what you want, but what God wants for you.'"

(Note: my term, *North Star*, is a synonym for God or a higher power, in case you didn't figure that out by now.)

"I later realized that I was just focusing on myself in life. I was chasing personal happiness, but the more I chased it the more it fled. I now understand that happiness is a by-product of fulfilling my purpose and making a difference in the lives of others. There is no other way of filling the void in our souls!"

Of this, Frankl said, *"Don't aim at success—the more you aim and make it a target, the more you are going to miss it. For success, like happiness, cannot be pursued; it must ensue, and it only does so as the unintended side effect of one's personal dedication to a cause greater than oneself or as the by-product of one's surrender to a person other than oneself. Happiness must happen, and the same holds for success: you have to let it happen by not caring about it. I want you to listen to what your conscience commands you to do and go on to carry it out to the best of your knowledge. Then you will live to see that in the long run—in the long run, I say!—success will follow you precisely because you had forgotten to think about it."*

## Sing Your Song

Some fundamental questions to ask yourself...

Why do I exist? Why am I working where I work? Is my work compatible with my life mission? Am I simply here on planet Earth to go through the stages of life, then die?

Or is there more to it?

I personally believe that you're here to do something only you can do. As trite as it may sound, your *North Star* put a song in you that only you can sing.

And if you don't sing it, both you and the world will be worse off.

## What's In It For Me? *Not!*

Be honest now...*are you living a life of "what's in it for me?"*

It's taken some people—including myself and that lady client—a lot of misery and a fair amount of time realizing that this life is not so much about us individually as it is what our *North Star* wants for us.

Some people never get it.

I often work with executive teams and married couples. Each "group" has its own characteristic problems, but the solution I give them is surprisingly similar. Using Frankl's great example, I cite his Auschwitz camp number, 119104, to remind them "to let go of your pride, readily forgive, stay engaged, become less selfish and find your purpose."

*This ain't about YOU...it's about what your North Star wants for you!*

The quicker you learn that, the quicker you'll enjoy peace and joy in life.

*"In times of crisis, people reach for meaning.
Meaning is strength. Our survival may
depend on our seeking and finding it."*

—Viktor Frankl—

# Problems Don't Stop
# Chasing You When You Run

I remind clients that a challenge won't go away until the lesson it's trying to teach is effectively learned.

What do I mean? Let's say you believe that escaping a bad marriage is the only way out. Or quitting a job is the only way you can find fulfillment.

Both could be examples of you running from problems.

But, again, problems like these won't stop chasing you until you've learned the lesson they're trying to teach.

I can't tell you how many people I've counseled who ran away from a problematic marriage only to end up with a far worse one later on. Or who impulsively quit a job only to end up with something even more disastrous.

Which is not to say that you should always stay in a bad marriage or dead-end job. There are conditions under which a marital union simply won't work, particularly when one spouse is investing a lot of earnest effort while the other just couldn't care less. And there are jobs that are never meant to be anything more than stepping-stones to something far greater.

But what I am saying is that decisions of this caliber should never be undertaken lightly, without serious and honest deliberation—and maybe even some professional counseling.

You should never run from problems.

At the risk of overdoing it, let me repeat that problems (even the most hurtful ones) have gifts within them.

## Meaningful Death

I guess the ultimate "problem" is death.

When we die, I believe we go to a far better place where we can still progress in the wonderful presence of our loved ones. That doesn't sound so bad, now does it?

It's when one of our loved ones dies ahead of us that we can feel a profound sense of loss, something that can be extremely hard to get over. Can we find meaning in an untimely death? Here are some comments I've put in question form that were made by my clients.

- Can death serve as a wakeup call to a more fulfilling life today?

- Can it serve to remind us to love and appreciate others while we still can?

- Can it teach us that we can actually get through our worst fears?

- Can it be the impetus for us to prevent or reduce pain and suffering wherever we can?

- Can it teach us to not take for granted the many blessings we have?

- Can it teach us to let go of the past and embrace what's next?

- Can it help us help others?

- Can it help us create a new vision?

- Can it help us be less judgmental and more forgiving of one another, and of ourselves?

- Can it teach us to savor the memories we create?

- Can it teach us to focus on the "big picture" and not take life so seriously?

- Can it teach us to enjoy the present moment?

- Can it teach us to let our love flow everyday?

Your response to death ultimately becomes your choice. The real tragedy in life is not that we die, but that not all of us live.

## Don't Make It So Hard

In life, many people make discovering their purpose an overly difficult task.

"Finding your purpose...creating your purpose... living your purpose"—the whole purpose thing can get pretty obnoxious.

But it doesn't have to be. Sure, there are countless books, DVDs, seminars and workshops on the subject, often using complex methods of identifying your life's purpose...when, after all, your purpose is to simply be in the "here and now."

> *"Ultimately, man should not ask what the meaning of his life is, but rather must recognize that it is he who is asked. In a word, each man is questioned by life; and he can only answer to life by answering for his own life; to life he can only respond by being responsible."*
>
> —Viktor Frankl—

Your purpose is realized when you choose to do your very best with whatever the moment is presenting you, whether it's good or bad. This very minute, the one right now, presents you with a choice of either growing and serving others...or taking your hands off *The Helm* and drifting aimlessly. A purposeful contribution is more about what you give today than what you take; more how you serve than are served.

Henry Golding said, *"What our deepest self craves is not mere enjoyment, but some supreme purpose that will enlist all our powers and will give unity and direction to our life. We can never know that profoundest joy without a conviction that our life is significant—not a meaningless episode."*

And that supreme purpose is usually, in my opinion, serving others.

## Finding Your Purpose *Made Easy*

So here's the million-dollar question:

What's the purpose of *your* existence?

Have you ever pondered that question for more than ten seconds? Oddly enough, most people I work with HAVE NEVER done that. Ever.

Why? Because it can be a pretty tough question to answer.

---

*"The meaning of life is to find your gift, the purpose of life to give it away."*

—Attributed to Pablo Picasso—

---

**PRACTICAL TIP:** It's time to do more PPP: PONDER your PURPOSE on PAPER. I invite you to take some time to "genuinely" ponder this question.

Here's what to do: Get a piece of paper and write about your purpose for at least ten minutes. Put it away and come back to it in two days, read it again and make the appropriate adjustments.

Lastly, re-visit it again in a month to fine-tune it. Then refer to it on a regular basis. Engrave it on your heart. Let it be your life's song. Let it motivate you to rise above every challenge and take you places you've never imagined!

I promise if you do this, you'll have more clarity in your life and more power to make better choices. And you'll be well on your way to achieving your purpose.

## The KISS Method Of Finding Your Purpose

Don't be offended if I suggest you *Keep It Simple, Stupid* (KISS).

I'm not actually calling you stupid. I'd never do that. That's just how the saying goes. Even so, it applies nicely to our "purpose-building" here.

The danger of making the search for purpose a big deal is that you can get stuck in the process and never get around to actually living it. Many get hung up on the *techniques* of big-time motivators: The particulars of their plan...the excruciating details...the monotonous practice...the scheduling of "what you're supposed to do," etc.

While these things are not necessarily bad in and of themselves, I don't want you to be, as Paul says in the Bible, *"Forever learning and never able to come to a knowledge of the truth."*

So here's what I suggest you do:

*"Things may not always turn out the way you would like, but you can always bring significance into your life by serving others."*

—Unknown—

First, develop the principles you want to incorporate in your life (and you already started doing that here).

Second, think how you can be of service to others.

Third, be alert to what surfaces. More often than not, you won't find your purpose...

...*it'll find you!*

---

> "The service we render to others is really the rent we pay for our room on this Earth. It is obvious that man is himself a traveler; that the purpose of this world is not 'to have and to hold' but 'to give and to serve.' There can be no other meaning."
>
> —Sir Wilfred T. Grenfell—

---

## Principles Govern Details

Again, your purpose *is based on principles*.

Principles have a different perspective than day-to-day decisions. Their timeframes are longer. And their intent is no-nonsense. An example might be, "I'm going to be honest in all my dealings."

Having principles is like that saying, "Never trade what you want now, for what you want most."

Principles dictate what you do on a daily basis. Not the other way around. At least for successful people. The accomplished individual measures daily decisions against the core principles he or she has assembled over a lifetime. That's what anchors them, keeps them moving effectively toward their goals.

On the other hand, too many people have too few principles.

They live according to whatever wind is blowing them that day. They let the details of the moment dictate their principles. Like the tail wagging the dog.

Ever hear of "situational ethics"?

This is, needless to say, a losing formula.

## The Moment—Where The Rubber Meets The Road

I'm going to make an assumption that you're already trying to apply your principles every day, am I right?

Not so good of an assumption? Okay...try this little exercise.

---

**PRACTICAL TIP:** This one will build on the purpose and principles you've already written about. It's aimed at helping you put your purpose into action.

Take a piece of paper and write down a principle you've practiced in the areas below during this past week (okay, use the last month if you have to go back that far). Describe under "Sentence" exactly what you did.

AREA PRINCIPLES SENTENCE (DESCRIBE THE PRINCIPLES IN ACTION)

- Family:
- Work:
- Personally:
- Spiritual:
- Financial:
- Social:
- Health:

---

Does that give you a better feel for the principles that basically run your life...or the lack thereof?

## Look Outward

Steering toward your *Lighthouse* always has a component of blessing the lives of others.

Frankl discussed this idea:

> "*Only to the extent that someone is living out this self-transcendence of human existence, is he truly human or does he become his true self. He becomes so, not by concerning himself with his self's actualization, but by forgetting himself and giving himself, overlooking himself and focusing outward.*"

*"If I have been of service, if I have glimpsed more of the nature and essence of ultimate good, if I am inspired to reach wider horizons of thought and action, if I am at peace with myself, it has been a successful day."*

—Alex Noble—

# Chapter 12

# HOW TO STAY AT THE HELM: RENEW, ENERGIZE & INVIGORATE

*"Meaning is not something you stumble across. Meaning is something you build into your life."*

—John Gardner—

I love going to seminars, reading books and listening to motivational speeches, but it all seems to wear off in a day or so. Tell the truth…you've probably felt the same way too, right?

You *want* to take the things you've heard or read about with you into the real world, but they often get lost in the translation.

So how do you do it? How do you "capture" good ideas and incorporate them into your life?

## Three Keys To Staying At *The Helm...*
## And How To Make Them Your Own

Motivation is great, but it comes with an awfully short shelf life!

Zig Ziglar was quoted as saying "People often say that motivation doesn't last. Well, neither does bathing—that's why we recommend it daily."

In this chapter, I'll share three Keys with you that have helped thousands of people stay at The Helm the rest of their lives. I'm sure these Keys will help you do the same.

The trick here is to make them as much a habit as brushing your teeth.

Remember, *you are your habits!*

Building lasting habits takes focus and a bit of work. Maybe you've heard that it takes doing something seven times before it becomes a habit? I've mentioned it earlier in the book, in fact. But it's not always that easy. In many ways, that's the "fast food" approach to habit building.

In reality, it takes focus, dedication and persistence to get habits carved deep into that brain of yours. And it takes time for all that to happen.

It's kind of like learning how to type.

When you first start out trying to type, with your fingers correctly positioned on the right keys, it feels hopelessly awkward. You have to self-consciously lift one finger, move it laterally a half inch or so, and put it on this key; then self-consciously lift another finger, move it laterally a half inch or so, and put it on that key. This takes a painstaking amount of effort and a seemingly interminable amount of time when you feel like nothing at all is improving.

Then, one day, your fingers start going where they're supposed to go on their own.

Ralph Waldo Emerson described the process of developing habits this way: "That which we persist in doing becomes easy to do; not that the nature of the thing has changed, but that our power to do it has increased."

But that's what it takes to build a great habit. There's just no free lunch in life. Okay...

# Key #1:
# Find Gratitude
# Within Your Challenges

"The flower that blooms in adversity is most precious!"

That's Frankl again. Somehow, this giant of a man found gratitude for the smallest things right in the center of hell! One time, he professed his gratitude for finding a piece of vegetable in the warm water the Nazis called soup.

Gratitude seems to be in short supply in our day and age. Sure, it's easy to nod and render a perfunctory thanks for something someone went out of their way to do.

Is that really heartfelt gratitude, though? Or more of a social custom?

When have you taken the time to really express the gratitude you feel? To really get into it?

Many Greeks carry around a string of beads called "Worry Beads." The owner is supposed to count each blessing he or she is grateful for, one bead/blessing at a time, until they reach the end, at which point, now filled

*"Gratitude bestows reverence, allowing us to encounter everyday epiphanies, those transcendent moments of awe that change forever how we experience life and the world."*

—John Milton—

with gratitude, the owner feels a whole lot better about their day.

It's interesting that they're called "Worry Beads."

Maybe gratitude is an antidote for worry.

## 119104s In All Shapes And Sizes To Help You Grow

It's hard to get too far down the road of life before encountering something that weighs heavy on your heart. That's whether you're ten years old or 80.

Maybe you're concerned about a relationship, whether you're a teenage boy trying to come to terms with the insane hormones swirling through your body, or a teenage girl trying to break up with just such a boy.

Or maybe you're struggling with a sadness that leaves you numb and empty (if you've been stuck in this place very long, by the way, consider getting professional help).

Perhaps you're worried about your finances and ability to stay afloat. Or the economy and your job security. Or the person at work who's just making you nuts.

Or the pains and consequences of a scary addiction.

Or maybe it's just the everyday boredom that's driving you crazy.

To a far lesser extent (most likely, anyway), we each have our own version of Frankl's 119104 prisoner tattoo. It's when we can feel and express gratitude for what we still do have, right smack dab in the middle of those trials, that makes us great.

And not only does that kind of gratitude greatly enlarge our souls, it can clear the confusion, put us back in balance, and help us see the proper way out of our troubles.

## Worry Versus Gratitude

One characteristic that differentiates us from all other animals is our ability to worry.

Yes, it's a wonderful thing to love and worry about the people we love. But if this nagging worry, this constant fear, always blinds you to the beauties of the day, then, let's face it, *you're way out of balance.*

Do you know people like that? Are you one yourself?

Are you so possessed by the concerns of the day, the suspense in life, that you simply can't tear yourself away from this miserable grinding attitude long enough to appreciate something nice  someone did for you? Or some beautiful landscape you see out your window?

That kind of worry alone can kill you.

The irony is, most things we worry about never take place. *"I am an old man and I have known a great many troubles, but most of them never happened,"* said Mark Twain.

Here's a sweet truth: *When you're humble enough to be grateful, you simply can't worry or feel stressed.* Just like, in physics, light and darkness cannot co-exist at the same time, so too can genuine gratitude effectively displace anxiety.

The light of gratitude dissolves the shadow of worry every time.

What weighs on your heart today? Whether it's a current problem that keeps you up at night or a nagging issue that's been dogging you for years, this gratitude, Frankl's 119104 example, can heal you.

Are you ready to be healed?

## Something To Be Grateful For

I'm not suggesting you pretend to feel terrific when you're not. You wouldn't want to be in denial like that.

If you broke a bone, you wouldn't suddenly tear off the cast and limp around pretending you're all healed now, would you? That would be way too painful.

You're healed when you're healed, simple as that. It can't be rushed.

But, along the way, you can still acknowledge *something* about the situation to be grateful about. Maybe you can feel gratitude that though you were in a bad car wreck, you're still alive. Or though you lost your spouse, your life was entirely fulfilled by the time you spent together and the memories you still retain. Or though you lost your job, you're now more qualified than you've ever been before to get a job as good or better as the one you lost.

This isn't Pollyanna stuff. This is genuine Greek "Worry Beads" stuff. If you take a good look, you do, in fact, have something to be grateful for. You do. And the Great God (or whatever higher power you look to) will spot that gratitude of yours and reward you accordingly.

*In my opinion, gratitude is the number one key to happiness.* The happiest people in the world are those who can find gratitude when it's seemingly the hardest thing to find. In fact, gratitude is always present whenever you come across happiness.

Let me make this guess: I'll bet that the people you hang out with the most are basically grateful, optimistic people who always help you recharge your batteries. Am I right? Grateful people see the bright side of dark situations.

Not the dark side of bright situations.

## You Don't Have To Be A Pollyanna (But She Wasn't All That Bad)

I mentioned having gratitude but not being a Pollyanna? Well, who was this Pollyanna character anyway?

*Pollyanna* was actually a 1913 best-selling novel by Eleanor H. Porter, considered a classic in children's literature. It's about Pollyanna Whittier, an orphan girl sent to live with her rather mean Aunt Polly. What rubbed Aunt Polly the most was Pollyanna's *Glad Game*, her attitude of unwavering optimism and finding the good in every conceivable situation.

Aunt Polly wasn't cut from the same cloth. True, she was wealthy and, true, she had her health, but she also had a sour attitude as thick as pea soup. And that clashed with Pollyanna's unsinkable sense of optimism. Once when Aunt Polly tried to punish her niece for being late to dinner by sentencing her to bread and milk, Pollyanna emphatically thanked her not only because she liked bread and milk, but also enjoyed the servant, Nancy, who brought it to her.

Okay, that's a little much, but so far so good, right?

In spite of Aunt Polly, Pollyanna's *Glad Game* is contagious, infecting those around her, from miser to invalid. The climax of the story comes when sweet, young Pollyanna gets mowed down by a big, old car and no longer has the use of her legs.

Here, finally, her optimism gets put to the test. Lying listlessly in bed now, no longer interested in playing the *Glad Game*, she is a shadow of her former unflappable self...when the townspeople she so affected with her former attitude, come to her rescue with stories of how she improved their lives.

Yes, the book has a happy ending (what else would you expect?). Pollyanna can now find gratitude that she still has legs. Aunt Polly finally melts under her niece's unceasing barrage of optimism, lightens up, and marries the handsome doctor while Pollyanna gets shipped to a hospital where, uh huh, she regains the full use of her legs (only now she's almost too overcome with appreciation to use them). End of story.

If you detect a note of sarcasm here it's only because Pollyanna, with her almost bullet-proof optimism, seemed to be more in denial than authentically grateful. In the real world, it's totally okay to feel anguish, sadness, dejection, even temporary depression for the tough things we go through. That's not only normal over the short-term, it's good for our long-term growth. And it's only what our Creator expects of us, I believe.

Pollyanna-types might actually be expressing a form of denial by not allowing themselves to genuinely feel the depths of their unfortunate conditions, when such a thing is entirely appropriate.

But it's the Frankls of the world (and you can be one of them) who sink to those depths knowing full well the situation they find themselves in, yet can still generate genuine hope, gratitude and appreciation in their hearts for what they still have.

Frankl was no Pollyanna. Even so, Pollyanna wasn't all that bad.

## Gratitude Turbo-Boosts Performance

Gratitude increases productivity.

If you don't believe me, just work with some ungrateful son-of-a-gun (if you don't already) who is witching and moaning all the time and see just how quickly they can drain the energy right out of you.

*Entitlement is the number one gratitude killer.* Need a good definition for that? How about, "the right to have something." In this case, these are people who believe they have the right to have more than what their efforts would otherwise justify.

These are the whiners, the complainers, the grumblers, in other words.

Simply put, whiners can dissolve trust and success like acid on fabric. These people are a real buzzkill to any organization.

Try drowning out the whining with gratitude and see what happens to your organization's productivity.

## Key To Happiness

Like I said, the happiest people in the world are those who can find gratitude every day, no matter the challenge.

I heard the story of a Marine coming back from the war. His wife had scrimped and saved to buy him the big-screen TV he wanted. He loved it, but not two minutes later, their 3-year-old ran into it with his Big Wheel and totaled it on the tile floor. The soldier's wife freaked out.

The Marine only smiled and said, "Hey hon, at least it wasn't a bomb! Nobody lost an arm or leg!"

Wow!

*Gratitude keeps you focused on what's most important in life.*

I want to challenge you to adopt this same "gratitude attitude." What's in it for you? How about...

- More patience

- More love

- More humility

- More faith

- More hope

- More self-reliance

- More courage

- More endurance

- More resilience

These are the fruits of gratitude. Pluck some for yourself.

## Please Don't Throw The Chair

At the end of the first counseling or executive coaching session, I always make a point of reminding the client that, somewhere in their particular problem, there's a gift only they can find.

That's usually when they want to throw a chair at me.

*"What do you mean? You have any idea how hard this ordeal has been on me?"*

I usually answer (note: this happens enough times that I have a *usual* answer), "No, I guess I don't. But I do know that life is trying to teach you something important. And I have every confidence you'll find it, learn the lesson and be liberated."

That's when they tell me to go to...*Helm*.

Eventually, most gain the proper perspective and thank their problem(s) the rest of their lives.

They realize their problems were an answer to their prayers—something that ultimately gave them the strength and insight to lead others.

Note I said "lead others." That's what these problem-induced gifts are there for.

As mentioned already, you're supposed to share the solutions you discovered with others.

## Get Your Own "Worry Beads"

Maybe this is new to you, but gratitude is a *learned* skill. One that takes practice.

In the absence of gratitude-practice, all kinds of negative mental illusions can take hold. Usually, they focus on the things/skills you don't possess. These illusions would have you believe *you'd only be happy if you had this thing or that*.

This can feed on itself and eventually turn you into a narrow, craving whiner with an obnoxious sense of entitlement (who, surprise, surprise, no one wants to be around).

And you don't want that.

Back to the "Worry Beads"...

PRACTICAL TIP: You don't actually have to get an authentic string of "Worry Beads". That would be great, of course, but they may be hard to find in the States (mine was actually bought in Greece).

My string has 24 beads. So, first chance you get, go out and buy a string of beads with about that many beads. Then here's what you do: The next time you're worried or unhappy or stressed about something, count off at least five things, out loud, that you're grateful for.

Count a bead for each blessing. Maybe you're grateful that you've had a peaceful night's sleep... or were warm, dry and secure all night long...or can eat virtually anything you want this very day...or that you have mobility, both bodily (your legs) and vehicular....or that you and your family members are healthy at this time.

You get the idea. BE GENUINELY GRATEFUL for what you have.

Undoubtedly your parents reminded you, at some point in your life, that most people in the world don't have nearly the blessings you have. One study a few years ago said that Americans live today like kings did in the early 60s. I disagree. I think the average American today lives way better than that. Kings back then didn't have cell phones, high-def TV or the Internet, to name just three advances.

It's hard to believe this, but it can take some people on Earth months if not years to save up enough to buy a decent pair of shoes. *When was the last time you were grateful for your shoes?*

The goal is not so much to list off as many blessings as you can (although that would be fine, too)—the goal is to FEEL GRATEFUL for each blessing you do mention.

It's not hard to do, not when you really think about it. I had a friend whose wife fell down the stairs in their home and broke her leg in two places. After being carried up and down those same stairs for weeks (by my weary friend), she was incredibly grateful when she got her personal mobility back.

Ever think where you'd be without your legs? Your mobility? Now that's something to really be grateful for.

Breathe it in, feel it, expand it, savor it.

Gratitude works.

## Catching Up On
## What Makes You Grateful

Sometimes using those "Worry Beads" to count off past things you're grateful for can be incredibly healing.

For example:

- "I'm so grateful I was given the opportunity to be assigned group leader over the project. It will be a great opportunity to shine and demonstrate my leadership."

- "I'm grateful for the smile from that stranger in the store today. It seemed to push my reset button after a tough afternoon."

- "I'm so grateful my daughter remembered her part in the school play."

- "I'm so grateful my sales presentation went well. I was so calm and focused on meeting the customer's needs that I forgot myself. It was spectacular."

- "I'm so grateful I was able to meet my financial goal and buy that piece of real estate."

- "I'm so grateful I was able to ask Jenny out on a date, and she said yes. It was a big risk but well worth it."

- "I'm so grateful I had the courage to ask for a well-deserved raise."

Again, the happiest people in the world are the grateful ones.

Good gratitude takes practice. Grab your "Worry Beads" and get to work.

# Key #2:
# Be Kinder Than Necessary

Some say that kindness and compassion have no relevance in organizations today.

*Ridiculous!*

Kindness and caring play *a major role* in establishing a family or corporate "ownership culture."

It builds trust and, in the workplace, an entirely appropriate kind of "business love." Could the world use a little more love? Mother Teresa put it this way:

*"It's not how much you do, it's how much love you put into the doing that matters!"*

*"Small things with great love...It is not how much we do, but how much love we put into the doing. And it is not how much we give, but how much love we put into the giving. To God there is nothing small."*

—Mother Teresa—

How much love are you putting into your life right now? Seriously. If you were to rate the intensity of your emotions in a given day, would kindness and service even be a blip on your screen?

Is there ever a convenient time to be kind? Sorry, no.

You can't think, "I'll be kind at 9:00 a.m. for 2.5 minutes." That's not how it works. If Frankl had waited for the appropriate time to be kind in the death camp, it would never have happened.

Kindness is seldom convenient. Let me give you another one of those Doug examples.

## Adventures In Kindness

Frankl witnessed such things as people giving their last piece of bread to others who were dying, despite the fact that they, too, were dying. Or, in the bitter cold, someone giving their blanket to another to keep them alive.

It's amazing what the human spirit can do once locked onto its *Lighthouse*.

On a much smaller note, I was at the Oakland airport and saw a lady who must have been 400-500 pounds struggling to move a double-wide wheelchair. She had to be moving a mere inch every 15 seconds or so. It was a painful thing to watch.

She happened to be going the opposite direction as me, and, sure enough, I was running late. *I'm certain someone will help her*, I thought as I passed her by.

When nobody did, I realized that that "someone" had to be me.

I asked if I could help her get to the gate. She looked up with an expression of thankfulness, and as sweat dripped off the tip of her nose and onto her ticket, muttered a quiet, "Yes."

It was all I could do to push her up the carpeted incline while holding onto the strap of my briefcase. After several minutes of that brutal workout, I saw a downhill slope dead ahead.

*Yes, welcome relief!*

They were doing a remodel of the airport, but, as I got closer to the slope, my relief suddenly turned to abject terror; the slope now looked more like something Evel Knievel, in his glory days, might have concocted. It was monstrously steep with what looked like a fenced-in dead-end below—*now why would they put something like that in an airport?* Before I knew it, we were rolling our way down, gaining velocity with a vengeance. I could only focus on braking with all my might, mind and strength now, trying my desperate best to prevent a runaway wheelchair.

I weigh 200 pounds; this lady must have outweighed me two and half times. That meant our momentum mounted like one of those cartoon snowballs chasing Wile E. Coyote.

The lady, now experiencing a kind of roller coaster weightlessness, said "You better slow down."

Yeah, good luck with that—we were building speed like a 747 on takeoff. To my horror, I saw that we were heading straight for the dead-end—a construction wall with a sign that optimistically read, "No Trespassing."

By then, I was sprinting just to keep up with the wheelchair.

She yelled, "Young man slow down! You're scaring me!"

*No kidding. I'm scaring me, too.* As much as my Herculean efforts allowed, I yelled, "I'm trying! The brakes aren't working!"

At the last second, using every available molecule of strength and adrenaline in my exhausted body, plus a gigantic portion of divine intervention, I was able to turn the double-wide just enough for us to miss getting splattered against the wall.

We finally rolled to a welcome stop. Trembling, panting, in a drenching sweat by now, my briefcase strap down around my ankles, my dress clothes looking like they'd been slept in, I heaved a sigh of relief for not getting us or anyone else squished and saw her looking up at me with giant, bird-bright eyes.

In a high-pitched, post-traumatic tone, she said, "Thanks, I'll take it from here."

As I was walking back to my gate, a wise guy who had witnessed the whole thing said, "Hey, maybe because of you, they'll put in a runaway wheelchair ramp."

Very funny.

*I challenge you to be kinder than necessary. Just don't hurt anyone in the process.*

In retrospect, even with our near-death experience, had I not stepped in, *how would this lady have handled that Evel Knievel ramp by herself?* Unless she had booster rocket brakes I didn't know about, she wouldn't have. It could have been a really bad scene.

My kindness probably did help her after all (the inevitable PTSD she got notwithstanding).

Look for opportunities to practice daily acts of kindness. Remember that movie, *Pay It Forward*?

Acts of kindness are indeed contagious.

By being kind to someone, you might start a chain of events that produces tremendous dividends of kindness along the way.

"*Twenty years from now, you will be more disappointed by the things you didn't do, than by the ones you did. So throw off the bowlines. Sail away from the safe harbor. Catch the trade winds in your sails. Explore. Dream.*"

—Mark Twain—

Do daily acts of kindness take sacrifice? Oh, sure, maybe a little. No question there was sacrifice involved in what I did (punctuated by moments of sheer horror). But you're a big guy or girl. You can take it.

**Besides, this is one of my** *sure-thing* **secrets of success.** It works in your broader life, even if you can't exactly see the connection between helping an overweight woman at an airport and making partner in your corporation.

*"So many people walk around with a meaningless life. They seem half-asleep, even when they're busy doing things they think are important. This is because they're chasing the wrong things. The way you get meaning into your life is to devote yourself to loving others."*

—Morrie Schwartz—

# Key #3: A Risk A Day Keeps The Failure Away

*"A ship is safe in the harbor, but that's not what a ship is meant for."*

—Unknown—

Anyone and everyone who's ever achieved a great measure of success has known the loneliness of risk.

That's because there really are no manuals written about living the kind of life you want. Which means you just have to write your own, page by uncertain page.

That's risk.

Even so, risk, to some degree at least, is healthy. It keeps us trying new things, is the gap between where we are now and where we want to be, and is how we exercise our faith.

It's key to success.

And, sure, I know that, on some level at least, it doesn't seem fair. You must leave the comfort of the things you know for the discomfort of the things you don't, in much the same way ancient mariners braved the big, mysterious ocean for the wonderful things they presumed were on the other side.

In a way, it's like having a competition with yourself. Who will win today? Nobility or passivity? Fear or courage? Remember, it's not courage unless you're genuinely afraid.

Risk is looking in the mirror and asking yourself, "Are you really going to live today or play it safe?"

Not that you have to go out and dodge trucks on the highway or anything crazy like that. Risk doesn't always have to mean taking big-time, all-or-nothing kind of chances. Great progress can be made with smaller risks, as well. Like speaking up in a meeting when you'd rather stay quiet and safe...or saying hello to that girl or guy you think is just terrific...or trying that bold, new sales technique your buddy did so well with.

You can actually equate reasonable, consistent risk with progress.

Beyond that, risk is a shot of adrenaline, one of the quickest ways I've ever found to revive your dreams. It can re-energize you emotionally and help you break free of a funk.

It's a rush.  A charge.

When you risk something, it's anything but boring.

One thing you're certain to find along the way is...yes...
*yourself.*

## "Little" Risks Are The Key

As I said, I'm not talking about risks like jumping out
of a plane, bungee jumping or anything nutty like that
(although they may certainly qualify, if you actually like
these sorts of things).

What I mean here are situations where your *North Star*
nudges you to do the thing you're reluctant to do. For
example, it could be a risk...

- To say what needs to be said

- To love regardless of fear of rejection

- To love someone who, by all rights, doesn't
  deserve it

- To stick up for what you believe is right

- To say *no* regardless of the consequences

- To forgive, come what may

- To be kind, come what may

- To volunteer, though you don't have loads of time
  or energy

- To say *I'll do it* to the thing you haven't wanted
  to do

- To apologize, though you don't really want to

- To trust again

- To let go

- To follow your dreams with all the uncertainty
  that brings

# Go Small Once Again

I invite you to take a risk a day. A small one.

How do you do that when you really don't feel like it? You simply *act*.

Don't wait around for motivation. Act first. The motivation will follow.

Next, ask yourself each day, "What will it take to get me out of my comfort zone?" When you come up with an answer, act on it.

A word of caution: Really do start small. Don't begin by taking huge, unmanageable risks. Start with baby steps and build from there. Otherwise, discouragement may stop you the first time you don't meet your unrealistic expectations.

How do you stay at *The Helm* day in and day out? By applying these *Three Keys* on a daily basis. They'll help you feel in control when you feel like I did on that Evel Knievel airport slope.

*"You have powers you never dreamed of. You can do things you never thought you could do. There are no limitations in what you can do except the limitations of your own mind."*

—Darwin P. Kingsley—

# Chapter 13

# SET SAIL— THE CALL TO GREATNESS WITHIN YOU!

Has the time come?

I wrote a song for my son during the tumor scare. The song has a very special place in my heart because it reminds me to trust my *North Star*, let go and just soar.

It's called *Eagle*.

He fell in love with the majestic bird when one flew right over our heads, with a 7-foot wingspan, no less. Time seemed to stand still as we watched this magnificent bird soar by with the beautiful blue sky, majestic pines and stunning Grand Tetons as the backdrop.

*Awesome!*

The idea for the song came while we were at the hospital; he said "Daddy, this is scary...but I can be strong like the eagle!"

Here are the humble, yet (in its own way and if I do say so myself) profound lyrics from the song (and, no, *I'm* not trying out for *American Idol*):

*On a ledge, you're looking down.*
*Afraid to fly, might hit the ground*
*You've got wings, but don't know why.*
*Afraid to try, you're afraid to fly.*
*But deep inside, you know you're an Eagle.*

*Eagle spread your wings and you fly high. You're*
*an eagle, meant to fly so high.*
*Fly high eagle*

*A distant voice, it beckons you*
*To trust the wind, it will carry you*
*You've got wings, you were meant to fly*
*Soar and touch the sky*
*And now you'll know the honor it is to be an eagle*

*Eagle, spread your wings and you fly high*
*You're an eagle, meant to fly so high*
*Fly high eagle*
*Spread your wings, now touch the sky*
*Fly high eagle*

I never said I was Paul McCartney or anything...but, like my son calling on the strength from within, you can heed the call of your *North Star* and become courageous, too.

There'll be times in your life when that distant voice will beckon to let go of the safety of whatever it is you're clinging to and trust "the wind" to carry you where it will. Then it'll be up to you to either listen to your *North Star* or ignore it.

But if you ignore it, it may be a while before it whispers to your heart again.

It doesn't matter what your current station in life is, there's more for you...but you'll only find it by soaring.

Even as you read this, I believe the spirit inside you knows exactly what I'm talking about. Your subconscious self wants to spread its wings and soar to a new level of greatness!

Still...

## The Phone Is Ringing, Will You Answer The Call?

I was in Charleston, SC in a hotel lobby waiting for the shuttle to take me to the airport. I was starting to get worried because the shuttle was late, and I was short on time as it was. It arrived, and I sat behind a father and son (by their accents they had to be New Yorkers). Apparently he was dropping his son off at the university on the way to the airport.

The shuttle soon stopped, the doors opened, and the son grabbed his bags and started walking toward the gateway of his education and future.

The dad yelled in a stressed, high-pitched voice, "Son, I love you. Don't cause me any grief. Look at me son. No grief. You hear me? Now get out of here." The son started walking down the sidewalk as the shuttle doors closed, and then the dad yelled, "Stop!"

The driver slammed on his brakes, wrenching the neck of everyone on the bus in the process.

He then said, "Son, what are you doing? I can see why you need college, you're not using your God-given brain. You didn't even give me a kiss. Now get back here."

The son headed back, gave his a dad a self-conscious kiss, turned around and resumed his journey. The dad yelled, in the same style, "Now get out of here, son. Look at me. No grief, you understand me? None. Now get out of here!"

The doors shut, and we drove away. I couldn't help myself—it was all I could do to keep from laughing. I have thought, of course, what it would be like to send my own kids off to college, but this was 180 degrees from what I had imagined.

Against my better judgment I said to the father, "Bet you've been waiting for this day all your life."

"Oh yeah."

"And it shows," was my reply.

"Today almost didn't happen," he looked at me rather soulfully, and I said, "What do you mean?"

"I work for Morgan Stanley. The date was September 11th, 2001. You know the story. At 8:48 a.m. Tower One was struck. The Port Authority told us things were fine, and we didn't need to evacuate. One man made a decision that saved my life and 3,000 others. His name was Rick Rescrola. He was the senior VP of security. He ordered the evacuation of all 3,000 employees."

"We evacuated and, at 9:07 a.m., our tower was hit. Chaos, panic, death, confusion, smoke, fire all ensued. They did a count of employees and found that a few were missing. So Rick decided to go in there and find them. He literally ran in while everyone else was running out."

"Knowing the full gravity of his actions, Rick called his wife. She happened to be watching the events unfold on TV, then her phone rang and she dissolved into tears at Rick's voice. He was okay! He was alive! Never in her life had she wanted so badly to hear his voice."

"He told her, 'Honey, please don't cry. Some of my people are missing, and I have to go in and find them. If anything should happen to me, I want you to know how much I LOVE YOU! YOU HAVE MADE MY LIFE. I love you so much!'"

"The phone then went dead as she watched Tower Two implode into that unforgettable plume of smoke and ash."

He then told me that all the major newspapers did articles on Rick's courage.

I was completely blown away by the nobility of this security man! For a moment, I was lost in my own thoughts, trying to digest what he had just told me. Talk about someone *Taking Life by the Helm* and answering the call of his *North Star*.

Some people say there are no heroes anymore. A man and a son on a shuttle bus tell a different tale.

I told him, "I'm glad I watched you telling your son not to cause you any grief. Thank you!" We pulled up to my Delta gate. The doors opened. I grabbed my bags and walked away.

Without missing a beat he said, "Get out of here. Don't cause me any grief, you understand me? None. Now get out of here!"

I looked back and, with a smile, said, "Can I have a kiss first?"

"Get out of here! You understand me?"

# Graduation Quiz:
# Three Questions For You

Okay, let's wrap this up with you answering the following questions:

1) Was Frankl a victim?

2) When you're at *The Helm*, who wins? Who loses?

3) When is the only time you can be in control of your life?

## Answers (Don't Peek)

1) Frankl *was* a genuine victim, but he did not live with *victim mentality*. He found enough meaning in his pain to do two liberating things:

> a) He personally grew and reached for the highest potential within himself by...

> b) serving, contributing and blessing the lives of others.

2) When you're at *The Helm*, everyone around you wins—you do, your family and your friends. What's more, the people you work with, even the Wal-Mart checker you smile at, wins.

When you're not at *The Helm*, who loses?

All of the above.

3) The only time you're ever really in control of your life *is at this very moment.* That's it. You can't be in control of the past. You can't be in control of the future...even the future five seconds from now.

You can *learn* from the past and *plan* for the future but *this moment* is where the rubber meets the road.

If your mental illusions can get you to live in the past or future—in either of those "time zones"—you'll feel absolutely powerless.

Sure, I recommend setting goals for the future in part by learning from the past...but you still need to execute them in the rubber-meets-the-road present.

## The Goal Of This Book

My goal is to simply help you...

1) *Take Life by the Helm* (direct your own thinking and make your own decisions);

2) Listen to and act on the promptings of your *North Star* (fulfill the measure of greatness within you);

3) Steer toward your *Lighthouse* every day (do the thing that seems impossible, but your *North Star* nudges you to do it anyway).

My aim is for you to never forget the big picture of your life, the bigger story of why you're alive and what your heart beats for today. You're here to live a courageous, adventurous and deliberate life, and this is only obtained when you're at *The Helm*.

So keep your hands on *The Helm*, listen for the whisperings of your *North Star*, and steer toward your *Lighthouse* by making a purposeful contribution daily.

## Ready, Set...

The seeds of greatness are in you to live an amazing life starting right now...the same seeds of greatness that the greatest men and women who ever lived possessed.

Remember to start small. And remember the words of the dreadlocked guru who sold me the mask of the sleeping prince. His message reminds you to wake up and remember that you're one of God's beautiful creations, here to do things only you can do.

There's a specific purpose for your existence.

Use the "Six Warning Flags" to keep you awake and aware of how you're doing along the way.

Understand that *Taking Life by the Helm* is a process that takes practice and not perfection. When you screw up—and you probably will—own it, feel it and move on.

## I'm Pulling For You Here

I'm not hoping. I'm not wishing. I'm not even crossing my fingers that you'll grab *The Helm* now.

I'M EXPECTING IT!

Your loved ones expect it, your co-workers expect it, even that checker at Wal-Mart expects it.

Most importantly, YOU EXPECT IT OF YOURSELF.

When you feel like giving up, I WON'T LET YOU because I'm here pulling for you!

Wake up, *Take The Helm* and rise to your own version of greatness.

May God bless you!

244

## One Final Thing...

"Get out of here. Don't cause me any grief, you understand me? None. Now get out of here and go *Take Life by the Helm!*"

# ABOUT THE AUTHOR

Doug Nielsen has over 19 years experience as a motivational speaker, corporate trainer, and executive coach. Since completing a Master's degree in Behavioral Science in 1993 from UNLV, he has been instrumental in assisting thousands of individuals overcome self-imposed limitations and accelerate personal achievement.

In working nationwide with audiences including Autoliv, Boeing, GE, Morgan Stanley, Proctor and Gamble, and Sony, Doug has helped participants learn how to gain control of their lives and to develop the motivation to consistently succeed personally and professionally.

Through Doug's experiences as a private practice psychotherapist and as a former COO, he has observed that organizations and individuals become easily stuck in reactive, conflict-filled, powerless states of mind. After a life-altering conversation with Dr. Victor Frankl - concentration camp survivor and author of Man's Search for Meaning - Doug discovered his own ability to "take life by the helm." Since that time, he has made it his life's work to teach others how to regain control and to be at the helm of their lives.

In 2008, Doug joined the top ten percent of speakers when he was awarded the designation of Certified Speaking Professional by the National Speakers Association. Doug was the 2011-2012 president of the Mountain West Chapter of the National Speakers Association. Doug was the 2011-2012 president of the Mountain West Chapter of the National Speakers Association.

The father of four amazing children, Doug renews himself through close family relationships, his religious faith, and through donating time to teach karate to underprivileged youth.

For more information on his presentations, training, boot camp and coaching, e-mail Doug at *doug@dougspeaks.com.*

To help you keep focused on maximizing your potential, sign up for "Take Life by the Helm in 59 Seconds or Less" for **FREE** by visiting his website: *www.DougSpeaks.com.*